INSPIRING COLLABORATION & ENGAGEMENT

SUCCESS
IN RESEARCH

INSPIRING
COLLABORATION
& ENGAGEMENT

JULIE REEVES
SUE STARBUCK
ALISON YEUNG

Los Angeles | London | New Delhi
Singapore | Washington DC | Melbourne

Los Angeles | London | New Delhi
Singapore | Washington DC | Melbourne

SAGE Publications Ltd
1 Oliver's Yard
55 City Road
London EC1Y 1SP

SAGE Publications Inc.
2455 Teller Road
Thousand Oaks, California 91320

SAGE Publications India Pvt Ltd
B 1/I 1 Mohan Cooperative Industrial Area
Mathura Road
New Delhi 110 044

SAGE Publications Asia-Pacific Pte Ltd
3 Church Street
#10-04 Samsung Hub
Singapore 049483

Editor: Jai Seaman
Editorial Assistant: Lauren Jacobs
Production Editor: Manmeet Kaur Tura
Copyeditor: Sarah Bury
Proofreader: Jill Birch
Marketing Manager: Susheel Gokarakonda
Cover Design: Shaun Mercier
Typeset by: C&M Digitals (P) Ltd, Chennai, India
Printed in the UK

Library of Congress Control Number: 2019944165

British Library Cataloguing in Publication data

A catalogue record for this book is available
from the British Library

ISBN 978-1-5264-6449-1
ISBN 978-1-5264-6450-7 (pbk)

At SAGE we take sustainability seriously. Most of our products are printed in the UK using responsibly sourced
papers and boards. When we print overseas we ensure sustainable papers are used as measured by the
PREPS grading system. We undertake an annual audit to monitor our sustainability.

Dedication

This book is dedicated to all those we have collaborated with throughout our careers and to all those future collaborators we have yet to meet. It is also dedicated to:

Billy, Liam and **Lizzy**

Ash, Tom and **Jen**

Sitkow

and to the memory of **David Reeves**

Contents

List of further resources

Activities

Checklist

Information boxes

International examples

Reflection points

Top tips

Voices of experience

About the authors

Julie Reeves is a Researcher Developer at the University of Southampton and, more recently, a Co-I on the BRECcIA-GCRF project. Prior to this, she was the Skills Training Manager (Faculty of Humanities) at the University of Manchester. She has been involved with the Roberts' skills training agenda since 2005, working with postgraduate and postdoctoral researchers and academic staff. Her academic background is in politics and international relations; her doctoral research was in cultural theory and international relations. Her newly acquired knowledge and understanding was put to practical advantage when she taught in Eastern Europe for the Civic Education Project, where she learned much about differing pedagogies. She is a member of the Chartered Institute of Personnel and Development and the Society for Research into Higher Education (SRHE). Julie met Pam through the project to create the Vitae Researcher Development Framework; they became co-convenors of the Postgraduate Interest Network of the SRHE and then they published *Developing Transferable Skills: Enhancing Your Research and Employment Potential* together in 2014. Julie was introduced to Sue and Alison by Pam Denicolo, Success in Research book series editor, at the University of Surrey. She has found the discussions about collaborating and engaging thoroughly inspiring and enjoyable.

Sue Starbuck has been supporting researchers and academic staff since 1998. Based at Royal Holloway, University of London, as Head of Research Services, with a wide and varying remit which includes managing a team who develop and support research funding applications, facilitation of cross-disciplinary collaboration among academic and research staff and support for early career researchers. She has also built up considerable expertise in bidding for and managing collaborative Doctoral Training Partnerships (DTPs). She is involved in designing and running research-related training and presents regularly at seminars and conferences on various aspects of research support, most recently around research culture and collaborative DTPs. Although Sue has collaborated with Alison on several projects in the past, this is the first collaboration (of many, we hope) with Julie.

Alison Yeung is an independent academic writing consultant. She has substantial experience of designing and delivering writing training to academics in various research institutions in the South East of England. Prior to working independently, Alison had been Writing Skills Teaching Fellow at the University of Surrey for seven years, where she had responsibility for the design and delivery of writing training for doctoral researchers. While her professional career of over 30 years has been in the teaching of English and the design of teaching materials, her doctoral research, which she completed in 2004, was in Systematic Christian Theology and Chinese Philosophy. This deep interest in understanding the differences, and indeed similarities, between cultures has served her well in her work to support doctoral researchers in today's international academic environment. She continues to be passionate about the importance of intercultural understanding in our higher education institutions. Alison first met Sue at the University of Surrey, where they found themselves as 'partners-in-crime' on several collaborative activities and events. Alison also met Julie at Surrey when she was introduced through Pam Denicolo as a co-author on the *Success in Research* series.

Acknowledgements

We owe our very special thanks to two people: **Dr Erin Henslee**, founding faculty member of the Department of Engineering at Wake Forest University, USA, and **Jo James**, Deputy Director of the Public Engagement with Research Unit at the University of Southampton. Both Erin and Jo generously shared their knowledge and expertise with us, not only contributing chapters but also providing invaluable comments, examples and ideas to much of this book.

We are indebted to the anonymous researchers who contributed Voices of Experience and have informed our practice.

We also wish to thank the following for their 'voices', feedback and advice:

Genevieve Agaba, Doctoral candidate, University of Bangor

Dr Yaw Atiglo, Postdoctoral researcher, University of Ghana

Dr S. Alireza Behnejad, Teaching Fellow, University of Surrey

Dr Tula Brannely, Senior Lecturer, Bournemouth University

The BRECcIA-GCRF team

Dr Zoe Darwin, School of Healthcare, University of Leeds

Dr Steve Dorney, Director, Public Engagement with Research Unit, University of Southampton

Dr Kate Giles, Department of Archaeology, University of York

Sarah Golding, Doctoral Candidate, University of Surrey

Dr Scott Lavery, Department of Politics, University of Sheffield

Claire Pickerden, Collaboration Development Manager, White Rose University Consortium

Dr Caroline Pope, SFHEA, EAST of Scotland Doctoral Training Partnership

Dr Matt Posner, Process Scientist, Excelitas Canada Inc. (ex. University of Southampton)

Dr Eleanor Ratcliffe, School of Psychology, University of Surrey

Suzanne Spicer, Social Responsibility Manager, University of Manchester

Dr Jess Spurrell, School–University Partnership Officer, University of Southampton

Dr Joanne Tippett, Lecturer, University of Manchester

Stefanie Thorne, Director of Business Engagement and Entrepreneurship, University of Suffolk

Sien Van Der Plank, Doctoral Candidate, University of Southampton, and the 'Beach Hut Brigade'

Dr Kathryn Woods-Townsend, LifeLab Programme Manager, University of Southampton

Special acknowledgements go to our collaborative authors (and co-conspirators) in the *Success in Research* series: Susan Brooks, Pam Denicolo, Dawn Duke, Sam Hopkins, Marcela Acuña-Rivera and Carol Spencely.

Last but not least, thank you to all our family and friends, and colleagues at SAGE who have kept us going throughout the process.

Prologue

Who is this book for?

This book is a response to the way the role of the researcher has altered dramatically over the course of the past 20 years. Not only has the context of research changed, but the demands made of researchers and the employment expectations held by researchers have also correspondingly altered. There has been a massive expansion of research in higher education, while the demands on those undertaking this work have similarly expanded to include, for example, demonstrating impact, exhibiting value for money and disseminating results more widely.

The career prospects of those undertaking research either at the doctoral or early postdoctoral stage have equally transformed, with the likelihood of researchers being able to pursue a traditional career within the academy quite low in many, indeed most, disciplines in many western countries and at least challenging for most, whatever their circumstance.

One of the main areas of cultural change during this period has been the need for a willingness among academics and institutions to be open to collaborative opportunities. In turn, this challenges institutions to actively encourage and support academic staff and researchers to undertake such opportunities.

The role requirements of researchers in general have been extended to include such activities as preparing impact statements, undertaking **public engagement** and entrepreneurial activities, working with industry or on industrial projects, co-producing research with others, and working within teams of doctor researchers. This has led to more informal learning and a wider range of skills development opportunities within academia. Thus, in today's research environment, competence in working collaboratively and confidently with others and engaging with communities beyond the academy have become a fundamental skill-set for all researchers. Fortunately, in many institutions, this general shift in the landscape, which has placed additional, complex demands on researchers, has resulted in training and development becoming embedded in the practice of research.

The connectedness of research in today's institutions compels researchers to consider the broader context, to demonstrate real-world benefit and to make strategic decisions about next steps. To do this successfully, researchers, from doctoral and early-career researchers to experienced academics, need to develop the skills necessary to communicate their research effectively across a variety of audiences. They also need the tools that will enable them to address global challenges, to access funding through cross-disciplinary collaborations and to engage with the public and policy makers, as well as corporate and non-governmental organisations.

These skills are rather different from those needed to conduct research and to have academic-only impact. For a doctoral researcher, collaborating on research and engaging the public may be new concepts. Doctoral researchers may not recognise the benefits (or requirements) of looking beyond their own 'project' and might even be in an environment that discourages any time away from the research project *per se*.

For early-career researchers or postdoctoral researchers, although these concepts are possibly more familiar, the opportunities and expectations may be different: they may be looking at collaborating and engaging with specific purposes, such as obtaining further funding, job-seeking or extending the reach of their research. Early-career researchers are also likely to come up against more competition for their time, especially if activities such as public engagement are not part of their appraisal targets. While different career stages may be motivated to collaborate for different reasons, the core skill-set around **collaboration** remains the same.

At present, not all institutions, or indeed researchers, recognise the significance of this skill-set, as it requires a culture across academia, government, business and the public that seeks and encourages these collaborations. Nevertheless, this aspect of the research role not only brings personal and reputational benefits, but is, we believe, set to remain with us for a long time and to grow, especially as research questions require more inter- or multi-disciplinary, even inter- or multi-sector, knowledge and approaches to solve them. As authors, we believe it is critical that not only researchers themselves, but those who manage and support them, recognise the benefits of these newer opportunities and take full advantage of them.

This book is therefore aimed at a broad audience. The primary target group comprises prospective and current doctoral researchers, as well as early-career and postdoctoral researchers, and we have written it very much with them in mind. However, it will also be of value to doctoral supervisors, line managers and Principal Investigators (PIs) of research staff. For those who support and provide training to doctoral researchers and research staff, the book will be an especially valuable source of guidance with respect to some of the more novel aspects of training provision, such as the areas of public engagement, policy influence, impact with research, enterprise and external engagement activities.

What is unique about this book?

In this book we recognise and highlight the opportunities inherent in the many, radical, changes that have taken place in doctoral education and the research environment. These include the extension of researcher activity beyond the project and into other areas, such as sharing information with the public and/or external bodies. These activities are not simply 'nice to have' additions but are rapidly becoming mainstream components of researcher activity. In our view, if they are not already, then they soon will be integral to the role of researcher.

We, the authors, have roots in different disciplines and between us have extensive experience (at least six decades between us) of researcher development, research management and external engagement with research. We are all experienced proponents of, and advocates for, collaboration in many of its various forms, including our own experience of producing this book. As practitioners, we bring a unique perspective; one that is built on observation, practice or **praxis**, research, thoughtful discussion and lively debate.

Being on the 'front-line', so to speak, of the changes in the broader higher education landscape, our positions afford us an exceptional viewpoint – one of both implementing and responding to change as well as witnessing the benefits (or otherwise) and implications such change is having on researchers themselves. We are, then, in the privileged position of writing from the perspective of those who facilitate collaboration and train others in the skills necessary to collaborate. We are also, as professionals, collaborators ourselves. Indeed, this book is an exercise in collaboration, which has brought together authors with different backgrounds and experiences, from different institutions and locations, who have never worked together before but who have used their skills to bring this book to fruition.

The overarching aim of the book is to demystify collaboration and engagement. To do this we will:

- Provide the rationale and essential tools for starting the process of internal and external collaboration, influencing and engagement
- Present a framework of ideas on where to start, and how to collaborate and engage strategically towards individual and group goals

- Encourage researchers to seek the opportunities available to develop this skill-set to make the research the best it can be
- Assist doctoral and early-career researchers in building their competence in identifying the value of these opportunities and being able to make a strong case to their supervisors and line managers
- Offer guidance for those who support and train researchers
- Furnish a rich range of examples, case studies, exemplars and voices of people who have experience to share.

In line with other volumes in the series, the book goes beyond being simply a 'how to' guide on collaboration and engagement. It exemplifies the conceptual shift that has already occurred within higher education and is set to continue, demonstrating to researchers, their supervisors, line-managers/PIs and broader institutions the benefits and advantages of collaborating and engaging widely within research. Importantly, as well as demonstrating the benefits of collaboration and providing practical advice and guidance, as the title suggests, the book aims to inspire doctoral and early-career researchers and those who support them. This it does by offering fresh ideas and in-depth case studies from the lived experiences of researchers drawn from a broad cross-section of disciplines and experiences, giving you, the reader, the confidence to take the initiative in collaborating and engaging with others.

The benefits for doctoral and early-career researchers of collaborating and engaging more widely are considerable, not only personally and in terms of well-being and current projects, but also for future activities and careers. We urge doctoral researchers, early-career researchers, their supervisors, PIs and **researcher developers** not to be intimidated by extra-curricular activities, but to embrace the opportunities that collaborations and engagement bring.

How can you make best use of this book?

Inspiring Collaboration and Engagement is not a textbook, nor is it a handbook. It does not take you from the beginning of a collaboration or engagement activity to the end, listing the steps you need to take on the way. Rather, this book takes you, the reader, on a journey of exploration through the terrain of collaboration and engagement, pointing out key features and offering advice on the way. It is a book of mentoring advice – the sharing of a range of insights and knowledge for mutual benefit.

We have made every effort to include international viewpoints and to be mindful that activity, and the potential for activity, will vary considerably both between institutions and between countries and regions. However, there are some areas where it has been pertinent to focus on developments that have occurred in the UK context, especially as they relate to doctoral training and public engagement. Our aim, in focusing on these examples, is to offer what we believe to be a useful insight on models of activity that you can draw on to develop your own ideas and, perhaps, even be inspired by to apply some of our experiences and lessons learned to your own context.

The book is not designed to be read from cover to cover, although, of course, it can be. We have written it to facilitate 'dipping in and out', and so chapters and sections can be read independently of each other. Where it would be helpful for you to refer to another section of the book, or indeed to a sister book in the *Success in Research* series, we signpost this for you in the text. For simplicity and ease of use, each chapter follows a similar pattern. Each begins with key points and contains a variety of boxed activities, top tips, voices of experience, case studies, reflection points and checklists, as appropriate, and closes with a short list of further reading. The voices of experience and case studies, which have been contributed by researchers and experienced practitioners, are included to help bring sections to life and to demonstrate the relevance of activities and opportunities. We are very grateful to the researchers, friends and colleagues who contributed these voices and have made this book inspiring through sharing and demonstrating the rich range of possibility in this area.

The book comprises three parts. Part I, *Engaging with the process*, introduces the ideas of collaborating and engaging with others and presents initial activities in these areas. It starts by setting the landscape and exploring why we might collaborate and engage with others. It then considers how to go about taking the first steps towards collaborating and engaging internally and externally and making the most of opportunities as they arise.

In Part II, *Success is in the detail*, we look at some key areas in greater depth. We focus on how doctoral and early-career researchers might collaborate externally and participate in public engagement activities or be supported to do so. Thus, it will be of interest to those who guide and support them, supervisors (titled advisors in some countries) and Principal Investigators. We also consider what can be learned from two recent UK phenomena, partnerships – the **Doctoral Training Partnership** (DTP) and the **Knowledge Transfer Partnership** (KTP) – and from Public and Community Engagement, drawing parallels between these and other activities and structures worldwide. Finally, we consider the possible benefits from these structures and activities. In addition to emphasising the value of learning from best practice and from each other through networks and collaborations, we highlight the professional skills that researchers can acquire through these kinds of activity.

In Part III, *Progressing with confidence*, we highlight four themes and consider them in greater depth. The chapters specifically explore building networks of trust, facilitating collaboration in a practical way, dealing with resistance and maintaining relationships, sustaining and reaping benefits after the conclusion of activity.

Throughout the book, we marry up the practical and the theoretical in a way that is intended to be both inspiring and informative, always bearing in mind 7Cs of behaviour that make up our code of conduct for collaborating and engaging with others:

1. **Compassionate** – everyone must respect others' perspectives and points of view, and welcome the disruption that other perspectives bring.
2. **Committed** – everyone must be committed to the working relationship.
3. **Curious** – everyone must be curious about other ways of thinking and doing, and why things work, or do not work, as planned or intended.
4. **Candid** – everyone should be honest and open with each other about how work is progressing and impacting.
5. **Creative** – everyone should embrace novelty, be adventurous, and play around with ideas.
6. **Constructivist** – everyone should be prepared to meet the unexpected as collaboration and engagement are active processes developed through all parties involved, making the sum greater than the individual parts.
7. **(un)Certain** – everyone should be able to manage uncertainty – who knows what the results will be! However, that is the fun of undertaking research and this kind of work in the first instance.

Voice and vocabulary

Throughout this book we have endeavoured to engage you in a conversation. We have imagined the reader in diverse circumstances and at a variety of research career stages and levels of experience. Therefore, we have drawn on many voices to ensure that this conversation recognises and benefits from a range of perspectives. You may find that you can identify the contributions of the different authors despite our editorial efforts to bring some consistency to the presentation. We hope that, rather than making this a disjointed flow of discourse, it makes it more accessible and enjoyable, inviting you to join in the debate and discussion about the place of collaboration and engagement in research.

In higher education, perhaps more so than within other professions, there are sometimes differences in terminology and a wealth of technical terms that might well be interpreted slightly differently according to context and even historical time. To accommodate these challenges to communication, we have provided a Glossary of terms, which is not composed of dictionary definitions, but explains how we have used the embolded terms in this book – our intended meanings.

Where possible, we refer to both forms of activity, that is collaborating and engaging with others. Although we view these as slightly differing forms of activity, there are occasions when the focus is more explicitly on one than the other, but our intention is that this does not affect your smooth reading of the book. Finally, we hope you will enjoy your excursion through collaboration and engagement and hope that you find this book to be an inspiring and valuable tool on that journey.

PART I

Engaging with the process

1

Why collaborate and engage with others?

In this chapter we invite you to consider:

- What we mean by collaboration and engagement in this book
- Why collaborating and engaging with others matters to researchers
- A rationale for why you should get involved early on
- Collaborative working and engagement within historical and contemporary contexts
- Four key areas where researchers may encounter collaborations and engagement
- What might be gained in general from getting involved in collaborations and/or engagement with others

This chapter sets the scene for the chapters that follow and lays the foundation for the remainder of the book. Throughout the book we address, both directly and indirectly, how collaboration and **engagement** inspire innovative and **impactful** research, and how this activity is beneficial to researchers, the people who support them, their institutions and those beyond the academy.

What is collaborating and engaging about?

One could say that intellectual collaboration and engagement are as old as the term *akademia* itself; the name of the olive grove in ancient Greece dedicated to Athena, the goddess of wisdom, and the place where Plato debated with followers and founded his school. We all benefit from sharing ideas and from getting **feedback** from others, no matter what level or career stage we are at. Philosophers and scientists in the broadest sense have always engaged with each other; indeed, this is how Socrates developed his discursive technique, the **Socratic method**, to generate new perspectives. Artists, writers and creative intellectuals have also long corresponded and exchanged thoughts with each other and been inspired by each other's work; think of the influence of Italian artists during the renaissance in the 16th century, or of Japanese print art on the impressionists in the 19th century.

When the scientific revolution began in earnest in the 17th century, correspondence and scholarly exchanges between 'thinkers' became an established and orthodox way for intellectuals and scientists, such as Issac Newton and, later in the century, Wilhelm von Humbolt, to develop their theories and to connect to the wider world. Indeed, Newton famously wrote in a letter to Robert Hooke (a fellow scientist) in February 1675: 'If I have seen further, it is by standing upon the shoulders of giants.' Today, of course, we have the internet and a variety of media with which to encounter 'giants', exchange ideas and develop our thoughts; yet while contemporary platforms may have altered the scale and speed of sharing ideas, encountering and corresponding with others, including less specialist and public others, this has long been a common activity within the academy.

In some senses, then, collaborating and engaging are not new. Albert Einstein had long-term collaborations with Leopold Infeld, Nathan Rosen and Peter Bergmann, among others, and yet he is more popularly known for his individual theory (which may have also been inspired by conversations with a mathematician friend, Marcel Grossman). It seems that collaborating, engaging and exchanging with others need not diminish your individuality, as with Einstein; indeed, we, the authors, maintain that there is much for individual researchers, especially doctoral and postdoctoral researchers, to gain from this activity, as we shall demonstrate throughout this book. However, sometimes collaborative working may not lead to equal recognition for all parties, often those most junior in a research collaboration receiving less acknowledgement. For instance, in 1962 the Nobel Prize in Physiology or Medicine was awarded jointly to the American biologist James Watson, English physicist Francis Crick, and New Zealand biophysicist Maurice Wilkins; their late colleague Rosalind Franklin was not mentioned in the work on DNA structure, leading many to suspect that some so-called collaborations can be exclusionary and fraught with unconscious bias, even posthumously. We hope that the increase in collaborative and public engagement activity signals a transformation in attitude towards doctoral and postdoctoral researchers and the emergence of a more **inclusive culture**, one in which all researchers can receive recognition for their contribution. We explore the question of working for, and with, supervisors and line managers or Principal Investigators (PIs) in the context of collaborating and engagement in the next chapter. The key point here is that the rapidly changing academic landscape is generating new opportunities for everyone.

Engaging with others, as in the form of encountering and involving other people, usually fellow academicians, is an established form of academic activity; however, collaborating on more equal and mutually beneficial terms, as we will use the concept here, might be viewed as a more recent form of activity. While distinct in some respects, what is common to both is the need for human interaction and relationship building. One definition of collaboration characterises it as 'an effective interpersonal process that facilitates the achievement of goals that cannot be reached when individual professionals act on their own' (Bronstein, 2003: 299). In many ways, this is the defining reason why individual researchers and institutions enter collaborative relationships. Indeed, a central idea in Lorraine Walsh and Peter Kahn's edited volume on collaborating in academia (2010) is that we now all work within 'the social academy' and that academic work, including research, is a form of social activity.

Undoubtedly, the pressures of funding and the need to diversify income for research, combined with policy initiatives and directives of governments, are actively encouraging collaborations between individuals, institutions, the public and industry. These pressures are also fostering the sharing of resources between institutions, sectors and countries, including the sharing of researchers. This has served to elevate and intensify engagement and collaborative working, and to take them to new levels to such an extent that for senior staff in universities, collaborating for publications and funding is part of normal activity in most, if not all disciplines. It would be very rare for a senior member of staff to have never cooperated, collaborated or co-produced anything (such as an idea, paper or module). We anticipate here that the 'social academy' will become even more sociable in the future and as the contemporary world elevates these kinds of activity to a whole new dimension; one that encourages researchers to make connections across disciplines and beyond the academy to other sectors and communities.

Although the imperative to collaborate, engage and disseminate work more widely does create exciting and new opportunities for doctoral and postdoctoral researchers, as we shall see, these social forms of working closely with others, collaborating and engaging, can bring new pressures and problems. For example, the rise of collaborative working since the late 20th century appears to have become more inclusive, perhaps evidenced by the increase in the number of people cited on scientific papers and by the increasing importance placed on being first author. Undoubtedly, with respect to publications, doctoral and postdoctoral researchers are more likely to be cited among the authors on a publication these days; however, their ranking in the order of things can often be quite low, leading, not too infrequently, to postdocs specifically feeling disadvantaged. We will explore some of these issues more closely in Part III of this book. Despite these kinds of challenge, it is, in our view, clearly an opportune moment to celebrate this activity, and to provide guidance to those new to venturing and navigating in these waters. In addition, the intensification of activity makes these areas ripe for consideration in terms of the implication they have for doctoral and postdoctoral researchers, and, in turn, those who support them.

We believe that much can be gained for doctoral and postdoctoral researchers, their supervisors, Principal Investigators, institutions and other organisations, from collaborations and engagement activity. Indeed, on reviewing some institutional impact case studies for the UK **Research Excellence Framework (REF)** exercise in 2014, one institution found that many impactful projects began life with the work of doctoral researchers. Collaboration and engagement activity confirm that the researcher role is changing right across the career levels and has greater significance to doctoral researchers, institutions and wider society, for instance, than the completion of the thesis alone. This point is cogently illustrated by the range of researcher Voices of Experience throughout this book and highlighted by the reasons for getting involved in Information Box 1.1.

Information Box 1.1

Four reasons to get involved

There are four initial and main reasons why we would encourage you, doctoral researchers and those in the early stages of their research careers (both within and outside academia), to collaborate:

1. You will generate far more ideas when collaborating with others than you will alone – you can benefit from standing on the shoulders of others.
2. You can share and distribute work between the collaborating parties. This means workload can be distributed, which, in turn, can further generate new sets of ideas.
3. It is fun, although it does require some skill to manage and work with others. These skills may not be familiar to you, but can be acquired or learned.
4. You can have greater impact and reach with research **outputs** and **outcomes** through your collaborative partners and contacts.

We will expand on these four key reasons throughout this book.

We, the authors, are of the firm conviction that collaborating at the early career stages will not only be good for you intellectually, emotionally and personally, but will also provide you with an excellent professional grounding that will benefit you for the rest of your working life. Whereas in the past collaborating with industry or charities or engaging with policy makers was viewed as the province of senior academic staff, now doctoral researchers and postdoctoral researchers are undertaking this activity and finding distinct roles for themselves in leading events, work and activities in these areas. We explore these developments in detail in the second part of this book.

Although we acknowledge the challenges this form of working can bring, it is also clear to us, as practitioners with several decades' experience between us, that the ability to collaborate and to engage with others beyond one's usual domain are, in this century, key to career success both inside and outside academia. Working collaboratively and seeking ways of engaging others early on in your research career, even if you do not remain in academia, will provide the foundation on which to build your future career. We will look at the personal and professional benefits for doctoral and postdoctoral researchers more closely in Chapter 5. However, there are some additional reasons, discussed below, for considering from the outset collaborating and engaging with others as part of your research.

What can be gained from collaborating and engaging with others?

As we indicated above, although academics have always collaborated in one way or another, the idea that they should demonstrate impact or the benefits of their research through engaging with industry or the public has arguably only extended across the academy in the past two decades. Being required to submit evidence of the impact and benefits of research is also a more recent development; at the same time, it is becoming a key requirement and a norm, certainly in the UK, where research is measured or assessed by a national mechanism such as the UK Research Excellence Framework (REF). Although some disciplines have always had a history of engaging with the public in some form or other (for instance, in medical and health disciplinary areas and patient interactions), and other areas have been more likely to engage with industry than others (engineering and chemistry, for instance), the notion of engaging beyond the academy in some other disciplines in the arts and social sciences may be a relatively recent phenomenon.

Interestingly, engagement with people and organisations outside the academy may frequently be initiated and led by a doctoral and early career researcher before a senior academic. Therefore, we would suggest that collaborations and engagement are **disruptive** of established and traditional academic assumptions about how knowledge is constructed, conveyed and developed, and by whom and when. This activity does not need to be hierarchical in the traditional way academic relationships are conceived, that is, led by the most senior member of the team; it can be led by newer researchers.

The contributors to this book have certainly found this an exciting space in which to be located and act, but it does challenge traditional power structures and concepts about research, the researchers' role and their relationships within the academy. In turn, this may create tensions in relationships, particularly supervisory ones, and we will address this matter in Chapter 10. Indeed, we are minded that the learning processes involved in collaborating should be disruptive because this is the source of new ideas and how novel ways of doing things emerge.

Without doubt, there is variation between disciplines in terms of engaging and collaborating with others. As mentioned above, some disciplines, such as engineering, will have longstanding experience of collaborating with industry, for instance, while for many arts' practitioners, this activity may be very new (although some, such as musicians, will have experience of collaborating in their professional life with performers and performance as part of their research). Indeed, it is not uncommon for established academic staff to have no experience of this kind of work in many subject areas or departments, and it could be the doctoral and postdoctoral researchers who open this space for their department, supervisor or PI.

Some forms of activity, perhaps more so in the Science, Technology, Engineering, Mathematics and Medicine (**STEMM**) subject areas than the Humanities, Arts and Social Sciences (**HASS**), may require additional funding for specialist equipment for certain forms of activity, such as exhibiting at open days, at science and engineering festivals or for engaging with school children, are some common examples. While all disciplines will need to set aside time for staff and researchers to undertake this form of activity, for some disciplines, such as those in HASS, funding or the buying out of teaching time may be more of an issue than for STEMM subjects. Where research funding is not so abundant, if you are not teaching, you may need to bring in other money, perhaps through consultancy activities, to cover this work (or be able to make imaginative use of your time, as illustrated in Chapter 9). Other disciplines may have a stronger history of demonstrating the impact of their research, notably biosciences, medicine and health, but the notion of collaborating or working with end-users as a genuine two-way process, which is what activity in this area entails, may be a relatively recent experience for many others.

No matter which discipline you belong to, what everyone has in common is that collaborating and engaging with others is a learning process – ideally a learning process for all involved. Paraphrasing Ronald Barnett (emeritus Professor of Higher Education), collaboration is 'pedagogical in character' in that 'those involved ... will ... learn from each other, and so, [in turn] tacitly, will teach each other' (Walsh and Kahn, 2010: xvii–xviii). An additional benefit, then, to the four reasons for engaging and collaborating listed in Information Box 1.1 above is for you to learn from others.

Adjunct to disciplinary differences are variations in **epistemic** outlook and attitude towards this form of activity across the world. In western intellectual outlooks, the individual thinker (disproportionately male and white) has dominated **narratives**, disciplines and awards. As Barnett notes in his foreword to Walsh and Kahn (2010: xvi): 'Nobel prizes are awarded to individuals, despite the team effort often involved.' In other societies and academies, however, 'team effort' is applauded and the **norm** (for a further discussion of culture and diversity, see our sister volume for supervisors: *Success in Research: Supervising to Inspire Doctoral Researchers*; Denicolo, et al. 2020). Collaborating and engaging with others, by the nature of the activity, requires the individual ego to take a back seat. This is not to say that individuals cannot flourish, grow and find self-expression within a collaborative project (as Einstein demonstrates); on the contrary, it is to be acutely aware that superficially apparent individual success is often achieved with the help, support and input of others, as you might see in Reflection Point 1.1.

Reflection Point 1.1

Who has helped you?

Think of a recent achievement and success you have had. It could be anything – from passing a test, completing a paper or chapter, to learning a new skill or baking a truly delicious cake. Consider carefully who, or what, contributed to your success and helped you along the way. This could be from a conversation or formal advice or teaching from a friend, colleague or tutor. It could be the result of reading instructions, watching a YouTube video or following a recipe or instructions compiled by an old friend or someone you do not know. Now consider what stimulated you to undertake the activity that led to your success or achievement in the first place. The more you reflect on the matter, does it seem that there are more people contributing to your success than perhaps you first imagined?

Seldom is our success achieved in pristine isolation – we all benefit from help at some point.

From the outset, collaborating and engaging requires honesty about one's intellectual environment and involvement, as well as the way ideas and activity are generated. It also requires the transparent acknowledgement of everyone's contribution. As in Reflection Point 1.1, this involves recognising the wider contributions others make to the successful outcome. Therefore, in addition to learning from others, you will, we hope, also learn much about yourself. We will revisit this in Chapter 4.

Another area of gain from engaging and collaborating is, in a quotation often misattributed to Darwin, that 'In the long history of humankind (and animal kind, too) those who learned to collaborate and improvise most effectively have prevailed'; to prevail is not only to learn how to collaborate, but also to *improvise*. What does this mean for researchers? In this volume, we will positively encourage your improvisation in the sense of being creative, having fun, testing out, experimenting and learning to 'play' with ideas (all the things researchers do best!) and, we hope, with a whole new set of professional friends. This kind of activity requires effort at establishing and maintaining networks and partnerships, as you will see as this book unfolds, but we insist that it should be enjoyable, and that the benefits and rewards are certainly worth the effort, as we discuss in Chapter 4. Building your network is an obvious advantage of collaborating and engaging with others, but as our guest author and contributor Erin Henslee indicates, in Chapter 8, these activities require establishing and maintaining good levels of trust between people. Other benefits and reasons for getting involved with collaborations and engagement might be to establish new relationships and new ways of working, or for reasons of personal, departmental or institutional prestige, or to grasp the opportunity to participate in an innovative and exciting project. There may be many reasons to be involved and, no matter what they are, it is essential that everyone is clear about this and shares their thoughts and intentions with each other from the outset.

A final reason to get involved with collaboration and engagement is that researchers are looking at a fundamentally different employment landscape than they were a decade or more ago. Collaborative working is an essential characteristic to demonstrate when pursuing careers within and beyond the academy. Take a quick look at job requirements and you will see variations on 'we seek a candidate committed to collaborative, **interdisciplinary research**', often modulated by wording such as 'a proven ability to do so'. This means you will need a track record of evolving experiences in these skill areas rather than a couple of items on your CV.

What do collaboration and engagement mean?

We define collaboration and engagement as two or more people working together to produce an agreed outcome, ideally and preferably one that has been mutually agreed. This may not mean there is an equal power relationship in any collaboration or even equality of experience, which indicates some quite specific characteristics need to be in place for successful collaborations to occur. We have isolated some essential characteristics in our Collaborative Code (see Information Box 1.2).

Information Box 1.2

Collaborative Code: The 7Cs of collaboration

Below are the 7Cs of behaviour that make up a code of conduct for collaborating and engaging with others. You can use them to consider how inclusive the research project or activity you are working on is.

1. **Compassionate** – everyone must respect others' perspectives and points of view, and welcome the disruption that other perspectives bring.
2. **Committed** – everyone must be committed to the working relationship.
3. **Curious** – everyone must be curious about other ways of thinking and doing, and why things work, or do not work, as planned or intended.
4. **Candid** – everyone should be honest and open with each other about how work is progressing and impacting.
5. **Creative** – everyone should embrace novelty, be adventurous, and play around with ideas.
6. **Constructivist** – everyone should be prepared to meet the unexpected as collaboration and engagement are active processes developed through all parties involved, making the sum greater than the individual parts.
7. **(un)Certain** – everyone should be able to manage uncertainty – who knows what the results will be! However, that is the fun of undertaking research and this kind of work in the first instance.

Collaborating and engaging signify symbiotic relationships; each requires a two-way process of communication and interaction with others, which is a distinctly social activity. This necessitates honest dialogue between parties, because neither involve using or exploiting other people, their ideas or resources. This indicates that the basis of collaborative working, in the first instance, is one of co-producing something for mutual benefit and broader gain, and this can occur within the academy, as we discuss in the next chapter, as much as with people outside it, which we explore in Chapter 3. Engagement draws on the same principles but suggests encountering others and 'reaching out' to communities and groups, who may be external to the academy, in ways which hopefully involve a mutually agreed outcome, although that need not always be the case. For example, some forms of engagement may simply involve the sharing of information by the researcher with the community, as we shall see in Chapter 5.

Therefore, for the purposes of this book, we accept that both forms of activity are social, inclusive and respectful of all contributions and contributors, no matter what the power relationship is. However, while there is a good deal of overlap between the ideas of collaborating and engaging, engagement (as we conceive it in this book) will tend to be with people outside the academy, and collaborative work can be both internal and external to the academy. Further to this, collaborations will always demand some level of mutually agreed way of working and outcome, while engagement need not. So, for instance, when a researcher reports their findings back to a user-group, although those receiving the report may have contributed some information or data and may be interested to know the results, as in health or ethnographic research perhaps, they need not have been involved in the research process beyond that point. In contrast, in a collaborative endeavour we would expect all parties to contribute to the research process, in terms of research design, conduct, analysis and reporting, as in traditional Action Research.

Thus, we have proposed that, while collaborating and engagement work have much in common, they may have varying purposes, lead to different kinds of working together with others, require different processes of interaction, and produce differing outcomes. Where there is co-design, co-production and co-delivery of research, there will be considerable overlap between both collaborative and engagement activity. This book explores the distinctions between these activities and offers examples both to illustrate the point and to inspire you.

Literature on collaborations also draws a distinction between it and the notion of cooperation, which we share here. We think of this distinction as the difference between 'for' and 'with'. If you are doing something *for* someone, you can be said to be cooperating with them, while if you are working alongside someone and doing something *with* them, you would be collaborating with them. Subtly, in our distinction, cooperation need not have the same level of commitment as collaboration.

Reflection Point 1.2

Cooperation or collaboration?

Consider for a moment, how you would define the difference between cooperation and collaboration? Can you think of examples when you have cooperated with someone and when you have collaborated? What distinguishes them for you?

Whatever the form of the activity, be it a collaboration or an engagement activity, it will always require having an active dialogue and, ideally, playing or working to the strengths as well as interests of the people involved (all of which implies that you know, or can identify, what these strengths and interests are, which we revisit in Chapter 4). You may encounter the attitude among colleagues in your department or discipline that this is something additional to research. We do not think about it in those terms; indeed, the premise of this book is to claim otherwise. We would take issue with those who see both collaborative work and engaging beyond the academy as a form of 'extra-curricular' activity and additional to research; rather, we see it, and encourage you, the reader, to view it also, as integral to the research process and central also to one's personal and professional development.

Certainly, this has been one of the key developments in public or community engagement, particularly in the UK. As our guest author, Jo James, indicates in Chapter 6, the idea of co-producing research with beneficiaries and end-users has moved engagement much closer to the concept of collaboration in terms of mutual benefit and co-design. While we believe that collaborating and engaging should be integral to the research process, especially for doctoral and postdoctoral researchers because of the range of benefits it brings, this may not make it easy for you to undertake or manage such work.

If you do engage in this type of activity, you will most certainly need to acquire a range of skills and abilities beyond those required for conducting research itself, such as research methods, reading, writing and presenting research findings in a scholarly way. The good news is that we can all always acquire new skills when we want, or need, to do so. The even better news is that everyone, irrespective of subject area, has the potential to undertake this kind of activity. There is something for everyone in this; collaborating and engagement do not require you to be a certain personality type.

What are the key activities associated with collaboration and engagement?

Here, we identify four main areas where collaborations and engagement are likely to occur. We also explore how they present different opportunities and afford a variety of learning/professional development experiences depending on what stage you are at in your research career. (We use the phrase 'research career' inclusively here to mean a short engagement with research, such as doctoral research, through to decades of working as a researcher. However, we recognise that the skills acquired through the doctoral process serve one throughout any subsequent career, whatever form it takes.)

First, and most likely to be encountered, are traditional academic collaborations and forms of engagement. These include the conventional opportunities to collaborate to produce publications and funding applications, to team teach and to develop new areas of research and research questions. We explore these opportunities in Chapter 2. Other areas of activity are external to the academy, discussed in Chapter 3, and focused on industry and a range of organisations, including charities.

This type of collaborative relationship takes **discovery research**, typically conducted in universities, and drives it towards innovation (or **value-added impact**). For these relationships to work, each side must overcome a cultural and communications divide. A third area of activity centres on policy, involving policy makers and policy influence. This can range from local government organisations to international policy, and is discussed in Chapters 3, 5 and 9. The fourth major area of activity is involvement with the huge variety of sectors of the public, people and their communities, which we explore in Chapters 5 and 6. This fourth area is a useful and major source of opportunity for both doctoral and postdoctoral researchers alike. Working with policy makers, the public as much as with other external organisations or business, will require the ability to communicate in ways that are understandable to all concerned.

Within each of these four areas exists a range of possibilities and outcomes, but perhaps what is most fascinating is the impact and influence some of the developments in these areas are having back on the academy. We explore some of these with reference to examples in the UK context. In Chapter 6 we specifically look at the impact this work is having on the doctoral thesis, and in Chapter 7 we discuss the effect that external engagement is having on the structure of doctoral support and university missions, to draw out relevant points that will be useful beyond the UK. All four areas (academic, external, policy and public engagement/collaboration) have an international dimension, which makes the world of collaboration even more exciting, especially for doctoral and postdoctoral researchers.

In the context of the modern world, research and the academy has had to respond to rapid economic and social changes. It has been accepted that today's most pressing research and societal questions are often best addressed by **inter-disciplinary** approaches; consequently, funding for research has shifted to support and, in some instances, requires interdisciplinary teams. In some ways research collaboration has been a side effect of this shift, driven by limited resources, making sharing a necessity as much as by the requirement and preference for interdisciplinary approaches.

The future of research seems to be moving towards confronting some of the more challenging issues facing the world, such as climate change, migration, food and water security, population growth and health, all of which require a range of disciplines to contribute their expertise if they are to be addressed successfully. Thus, the need to cultivate the abilities required to build multi-disciplinary and international partnerships becomes more acute. Accompanying the opportunities in these areas are increased expectations that researchers demonstrate to the government and the public – their ultimate funders – the tangible impact of their research.

While funding mechanisms move towards collaborative, interdisciplinary research, the rewards and recognition structure within the academy remains embedded in the paradigm of solitary scholarship, such as individual publication rates and the quantity of personal funding income. This can lead to some of the resistance we speak of in Chapter 10. While we wait for institutional structures to realign with contemporary challenges and changes, we believe that the skills developed and honed through collaborating and engaging with others, particularly those outside one's disciplinary area and 'comfort zone', are likely to be in demand and become the basic characteristics of research roles both within academia and in other sectors.

The goal posts in higher education are shifting and expanding, so whatever experiences doctoral and postdoctoral researchers can obtain during their research period will be of great advantage and career benefit, as Voice of Experience 1.1 indicates.

Voice of Experience 1.1

Doctoral researcher on an international collaborative project

Working in a large international collaboration with over four country partners has great opportunities for the doctoral researcher but may have implications for creativity and time management.

Of course, as a doctoral researcher, I had the great benefit of access to funding to cover tuition, monthly stipends, and to attend international conferences and workshops

(Continued)

and to purchase academic materials. There was also a large pool of seasoned international researchers to interact with and to be mentored by.

Typically, international consortia have more scientists than doctoral researchers, who double as research assistants. I was recruited about a year earlier than other doctoral researchers and I served as research assistant for different work packages, including the geophysical sciences, even as a social researcher. It meant that I had many line managers who required my regular assistance, something that was enlightening but quite challenging!

I learnt the functions of work packages and gained a thorough understanding of the consortium research and these experiences helped me to adopt a multidisciplinary approach to my own research. There were early-career researchers who helped me conceptualise my research and gave me useful materials. I also had to prioritise work packages to reduce the pressure from line managers.

The research objectives of the consortium are predefined. Therefore, while the doctoral research must be aligned with the overall objectives, care must be taken not to duplicate consortia deliverables in the doctoral dissertation.

The research included a quantitative survey instrument, which was standardised across the three countries' sites and centralised by the lead institution. Hence, I had minimal influence on the instrument irrespective of the concerns I had. This meant, I had to redefine my research questions and adapt the available data to suit my research.

However, I got the opportunity to coordinate and supervise household surveys across different districts in Ghana, learning and extending many skills along the way.

Dr Yaw Atiglo, Postdoctoral researcher, University of Ghana

Both collaborative working and engagement activity require the mutual agreement and consent of everyone involved, even if this is only visible at the ethical approval stage for research and when consent is required to work with others. Collaborative working goes one step further by building on any mutual agreements and suggesting a stronger relationship, one that also implies an equitable relationship in some respects. In Activity 1.1 you are invited to review a list of activities, some of which, although they all involve an element of collaboration, afford stronger forms than others. So, the format this activity takes will vary hugely, which is good news as it means not only can everyone undertake this activity, but you can choose what would suit you best.

Activity 1.1

Is this a collaborative relationship?

Consider the activities below from the perspective of a doctoral or early-career researcher, and, according to the approach of this chapter, rate the extent to which they are collaborative, where 1 is not at all and 5 is highly collaborative:

- Writing a paper with your supervisor/line manager, where they are the lead author:
  1 – 2 – 3 – 4 – 5

- Writing a paper with your supervisor/line manager, where you are the lead author:
  1 – 2 – 3 – 4 – 5

- Working as a researcher as part of an international partnership:
  1 – 2 – 3 – 4 – 5

- Working with a charity to solve a problem with them:
  1 – 2 – 3 – 4 – 5

- Working with a schoolteacher to design a module for their class using your research project:
  1 – 2 – 3 – 4 – 5

- Working with a group of peers to design and deliver an interactive exhibition based on your research:
  1 – 2 – 3 – 4 – 5

Look at the list again. Although many of the situations will be determined by both the context and personalities involved, some, such as the first three points, might be more cooperative than collaborative. To assist with establishing the nature of the relationship, ask yourself the following questions:

- Does everyone, especially the researcher, have an equal voice?
- Whose idea originated the activity?
- Who developed it?
- Who benefits the most from this?

If the answers are along the lines of 'we all developed this, we all benefit (albeit differently), and everyone's voice is valued', it is more likely to be a collaborative effort.

For the authors, collaborative working and engaging with others has added dimensions beyond the common academic discourse, to the realms of industry, charities, schools, end-users of research and all manner of interested parties. Indeed, it is often in these other spaces that doctoral and early-career researchers are empowered, finding freedom to articulate their research voices and to form mutual partnerships and projects independent of supervisors and PIs. We will explore these wider landscapes in later chapters. Here, we suggest that the opportunities offered through traditional academic activity within your institution are a good place to begin your adventures in both collaborative working and engagement, perhaps with small initial steps. Chapter 2 addresses these.

Further reading

Bronstein, L.R. (2003) A model for interdisciplinary collaboration. *Social Work*, 48(3): 297–306.

Cooper, A. (2013) International success depends on collaboration, not just competition. *The Guardian*, 28 January. www.theguardian.com/higher-education-network/blog/2013/jan/28/internationalisation-higher-education-student-experience (accessed 5 May 2019).

Denicolo. P., Duke. D. and Reeves. J. (2020) *Success in Research: Supervising to Inspire Doctoral Researchers*. London: SAGE.

Glynn, D. (2016) Why early career researchers should care about public engagement. *Times Higher Education*, www.timeshighereducation.com/blog/why-early-career-researchers-should-care-about-public-engagement (accessed 5 May 2019).

Richards, M., Elliott, A., Woloshyn, V. and Mitchell, C. (2001) *Collaboration Uncovered: The Forgotten, the Assumed, and the Unexamined in Collaborative Education*. Westport, CT: Bergin & Garvey.

Stein, A. and Daniels, J. (2017) *Going Public: A Guide for Social Scientists*. Chicago, IL: University of Chicago Press.

Walsh, L. and Kahn, P. (eds) (2010) *Collaborative Working in Higher Education: The Social Academy*. New York and London: Routledge.

2

From small beginnings: what opportunities exist internally?

In this chapter we invite you to consider:

- Existing resources and opportunities within your institution
- Leveraging the opportunities presented by research, teaching and your peers
- Some examples and advice on how you might benefit from these opportunities
- How you can manage the small steps and initial foray into collaborating and engaging with others

Learning to collaborate and engage with others is integral to what it means to be a researcher. Researchers who lead large collaborative projects or who engage on the global stage will all have started out as doctoral and postdoctoral researchers like you. This chapter explores some of the ways in which you can begin to 'experiment' and 'play' with collaboration and engagement within the safe space of your own institution.

Why start small?

There is an adage: 'Go big or go home', which exhorts you to be extravagant, profligate and excessive in your ambition. However, when it comes to your first collaboration or engagement activity, starting small will be your best first step to establishing a good reputation and developing appropriate skills. You will find that there are lots of personal and professional benefits to this kind of work, as we discuss in Chapter 4. One of the features of higher education that we most like to celebrate is the fact that institutions provide an incredible range of opportunity in ways that no other sector does. This is something we hope to convince you of throughout this book.

Your immediate circle of research activity will be the first place to look for collaborative and engagement experience. Indeed, you are already engaging with your colleagues in the traditional academic sense of discussing and sharing ideas. For doctoral and postdoctoral researchers, your fellow research colleagues in a subject area, group or department will provide a rich initial source of engagement activity. The other key source of such experience derives from your interactions with your supervisor or Principal Investigator (PI). Yet, as we pointed out in Chapter 1, engaging with your supervisor or PI is not the same as collaborating with them. This latter form of activity may only emerge once you have developed your professional know-how further. The fundamental academic practice of exchanging and interacting with others will help you to build your experience and confidence to venture further in becoming an independent researcher.

Initial steps

Acquiring a new professional skill or understanding takes time and is an iterative process. What perhaps begins with a conversation with a fellow researcher in your department may lead you both to arrange a departmental seminar session. This, in turn, could lead on to a regular or larger presentation series, and eventually an internal conference. Never underestimate the value of small things, be they chance conversations or the opportunity to do a small favour for a colleague, such as talking about your research to their students. These activities not only foster the development of your professional and academic skill-set, but also begin to build your reputation as a member of a research community. Moreover, they will extend your network and, by working with someone else, your team working, leadership and management skills as well. The fellow researcher with whom you engaged in conversation and then who helped you to organise a seminar that has become a series of seminars, is no longer just a fellow researcher: they have become a collaborator, and you are now in a collaborative relationship or partnership. There may only be two of you in the 'seminar series collaboration', but this is how it all begins.

Connecting and engaging with fellow academicians, or building networks, is the lifeblood of academia. Networks are vital in finding funding, positions and potential collaborators for all kinds of activities. Taking every opportunity to meet with peers and colleagues will help to develop your network, as we advise in

Top Tips 2.1. We explore the role of networks in collaboration and engagement in more detail in Chapter 8.

Top Tips 2.1

Getting your network started

Here are some suggestions that include a variety of opportunities for you to engage with potential collaborators and to build your network:

1. **Attend your induction**. Even if you are familiar with your university because of a previous role, there will be something or someone new to meet at your induction. Perhaps you are the person who can be of help to someone else who is new!
2. **Make sure you update your email lists**. Chances are that you will be on default email lists in your institution, but make sure you look outside this and find other mailing lists or interest groups to subscribe to. Ask your veteran departmental colleagues for suggestions.
3. **Attend seminars and training**. These can be a great resource for meeting people outside your department.
4. **Give yourself time**. You will need time to develop your ideas and to pursue them. Networking via email lists and special interest groups, having conversations over coffee or in the corridor and getting to know people and their interests is time well spent.
5. **Be open and alert**. You should always be vigilant and alert to opportunities to get involved. If you are not certain about how to take advantage of them, you can always ask the people you have met through some of the previous suggestions.

From these small initial acts, you will grow in confidence and begin to establish a network of potential future collaborators. It is this pool you can draw from when you start taking on larger ideas, such as applying for your university's collaborative project fund or creating a team for a collaborative research paper.

Existing opportunities

Universities always have a plethora of activities and events going on, and every department will have talks and programmes for students and staff. Higher education is brimming with creative and new activities, events and projects, although those involved may not recognise the creativity themselves. In addition, universities will have services and built-in mechanisms, such as committees and training and internal funding schemes, to support all this fecund activity. Your first act in moving into a wider engagement and collaborative territory is to gather information about what is available that can either facilitate or support you. Surveying your institutional terrain and departments will help you to identify existing opportunities. You can then filter this information based on your own interests and requirements.

If you are being vigilant to those email lists you signed up for at induction, these can be a useful source of information. You can also ask those immediate to you if there is anyone in your department who is involved in a collaborative project or who has contact with people who are. What can your supervisor, line manager or PI tell you? It is also worth asking your fellow doctoral and postdoctoral researchers if they know and have contact with anyone, as quite often researchers have the most useful and surprising network and contacts.

Institutional opportunities

Starting small within your institution might simply be joining a postgraduate researcher group run through your student union. You do not have to start off running for an officer position; showing up to a meeting is an adequate first start. Another small start would be attending a regular seminar series in your department or the wider faculty. You do not have to say anything or ask any questions; it is simply important to be seen regularly until you feel sufficiently confident to engage more fully. You could volunteer to be a committee representative for your department or perhaps offer to be a participant for a focus group run by another researcher. While these are not, by our definition, collaborating opportunities, they are the small steps that begin building your network and self-confidence for collaboration to take place. The committee meeting you attend could lead to a future working group, which, in turn, could lead towards policy change within your institution.

At your institution there will undoubtedly be a variety of workshops, funding schemes, conferences or departmental seminars that contribute to the research culture. Some institutions may offer Public/Community engagement training and events. Disciplines, such as health and medicine, may have established connections with local charities, user groups or hospitals already that can provide you with proven routes into activity. Others, such as engineering, chemistry and electronics, may have strong connections with industry and perhaps hold regular commercial seminars or offer **internships**, **placements** or secondments. Arts- and Humanities-based disciplines are very likely to have connections with the creative industries, museums, galleries, performers and artists. We will explore some of the wider opportunities supported within institutions in the next chapter. First, though, Activity 2.1 invites you to reflect on ways you can connect with others within your own institution.

Activity 2.1

What opportunities exist in your institution?

Make a list of the opportunities you are aware of within your institution for:

- Representing your researcher community
- Representing your department
- Learning about other research in your department or institution
- Meeting other researchers in your department and institution
- Training and development
- Getting involved in someone else's research (do not forget to include those leaflets on the back of toilet doors!)

Once you have made a list, ask your colleagues, supervisor or PI for ideas to add to it.

Opportunities through research

Your research will generate a wide range of opportunities, many of which will take you beyond your institution, as they should. In this chapter, we maintain a local focus and list some of the key internal opportunities for engagement and collaboration below. These activities do not stand alone; there will always be institutional and departmental support and advice for you to draw on.

Research seminars

Your first collaboration as a doctoral researcher, as mentioned above, could be with a fellow researcher in your department or Faculty to arrange a lunch-time seminar session for fellow doctoral researchers. This is a useful form of peer support, and there would be no need to invite established academic staff. Indeed, it may be an advantage not to, so that you and your peers can build confidence and try out questioning and chairing techniques without the pressure or embarrassment of Faculty staff watching. It would, though, also be beneficial to find an empathetic member of staff to attend or observe so that they can provide advice, guidance and feedback on performance or act as chair if needed.

Stepping outside your department or subject area to invite and include research-ers from other disciplines or departments to join you in a seminar obliges you to collaborate with at least one other person in those areas. By including research-ers from other disciplines, you will have created an interdisciplinary event. Now you are on your way to collaborating across disciplinary boundaries and depart-mental divides – and this is where the exciting research projects and innovative approaches to problem solving are likely to be found.

Papers, journal articles and projects

Collaborating with like-minded others to write a paper or project proposal is creative and fun. If you are in a large research team, you may find you are con-tributing to group papers as a matter of course. However, this will be someone else's paper, journal article or project. As an up-and-coming research professional, you should look for ways in which to develop your own research interests and track record. This need not always be directly related to your research; papers can come from any aspect of activity that you are involved in and interests you. For instance, there may be a paper or project that results from your now interdisci-plinary seminar series or from your teaching experience or training methods (see Information Box 2.1). The idea is to obtain or leverage more from any activity and use it to your advantage. Consider Voice of Experience 2.1 from one of our book series' authors and then the ideas in Information Box 2.1.

Voice of Experience 2.1

Academic multi-tasking

It does seem that being an academic is a demanding, multi-faceted role. I learned quickly that the best way for me to cope was by ensuring that just about every task I undertook served at least two purposes. For instance, a conference is an oppor-tunity to present a paper, to meet new colleagues, to reinforce current network links and to chat up publishers; giving a presentation to the researchers in another university provides opportunities to share resources and find out what is going on in a national interest group and distribute flyers for our latest book. That this is a common academic ploy becomes clear when you attend a university or faculty meeting – everyone has their diaries out ready to book appointments with others or to request a colleague's support for a teaching or research endeavour.

An academic author

Information Box 2.1

Using training to produce a research paper

One of your authors was approached by a group of postdocs who wanted training in Matlab. She did not have any knowledge or experience of this software, so asked them to conduct a needs analysis and to put a proposal together. They duly did so and identified an appropriate trainer. One of the conditions of paying for the training workshop was an **evaluation** at the end of the process. This did not mean a reaction or 'happy sheet', but hard evidence of learning and behaviour change. The postdocs devised a test that they applied before and after the training event. They analysed the results and then went on to write a collaborative paper on their findings. (For further details see van Besouw et al., 2013)

Writing papers collaboratively, as the postdoctoral researchers did in Information Box 2.1, is an excellent experience to participate in. Simmons and Singh (2019) advise writing with others, whether that is 'on a regular basis with one or two colleagues' or in a larger group at a writing retreat, as it can be more productive and enjoyable than writing on your own. Our next Voice of Experience 2.2 illustrates how this process also evolves.

Voice of Experience 2.2

Collaborative writing

Collaborating with a colleague or several colleagues on writing a paper or book is an interesting experience. It is a relationship where you can see the levels of trust building up between you.

In the early stages, as a doctoral researcher, I found I was a bit inhibited in giving feedback or taking a lead on things. Phrasing criticism was an issue – if I was collaborating with a senior colleague, I would worry about how to tell them that they should do this or that, or that something was missing. One Prof, to whom I gave feedback on a chapter, told me I had missed his point – I was mortified! Now, I would probably question him again because his point was not clear. Then, as I moved on in my career, if I was working with a less experienced colleague, I would worry about upsetting them. Nowadays, I have a stock of set phrases that I hope work for everyone – 'this would benefit from', and 'I suggest we do X here…' and I always try to be nurturing in my approach.

As time goes on and deadlines approach, you find that you are batting text, drafts, chapters, etc., back and forth between the collaborators. It is at this stage that you can really tell if a good level of trust has been established. The tighter the deadline, the more I trust others, and I have also found that my inhibitions go out the window!

(Continued)

What I have learned is that someone always must take a lead and boss people about, or simply remind them of what to do next. I am not sure what it is like in other disciplines, but in my area that does not have to be the most senior person. In fact, it is probably better to have someone who is simply good at organising things instead, and quite often that is a doctoral researcher.

Researcher and Senior Teaching Fellow – Education

Finally, if you design or want to establish a collaboration based on research, which is also something all researchers should aspire to, you will need to take advantage of the opportunities you identified in Activity 2.1 and those provided by your university research/researcher support services, such as Research Management, Researcher Development, Research Innovation services or your **Doctoral College** or School.

Opportunities through teaching

You may have the opportunity to teach at your institution. Indeed, many doctoral researchers are obliged to demonstrate in labs or to tutor seminars as part of their programme. All forms of teaching provide the chance for you to work with others. In HASS areas, this may be working primarily with the module leader. However, some of your peers may be teaching the same course, which could provide opportunities for you to share best practice and ideas (who knows, there may even be a paper or seminar in it). We are aware that postdoctoral researchers are frequently denied teaching opportunities; however, this is where public engagement activity (discussed in Chapter 5) can be most useful. Often, engagement activity will demand the same or similar pedagogic processes of design, delivery and assessment or evaluation.

Working with others to develop lectures or teaching materials (which you can volunteer for) will be highly rewarding for you as well as for the students. Teaching will also provide evidence of your 'track record', which employers look for, because you will develop your ability to communicate with broad audiences and to give feedback to people. It will provide evidence of how you collaborate across departments or levels within your institution. If a team of researchers is teaching or demonstrating for large groups of students, you will be able to cite the way you manage the process between yourselves as evidence of organisation and leadership skills, all of which help to build your reputation for working with others. An example is provided in Information Box 2.2.

Information Box 2.2

Internal collaboration for outward impact

A doctoral researcher had previously worked at a museum before embarking on his research project. Using this connection, he and fellow doctoral researchers approached the museum about organising a family day of activity. The doctoral researchers then worked with a group of undergraduates to design and deliver a family day of events at the museum. What was inspiring about this project was that the departmental academic staff did not have the contacts or experience of running such events, although they did support the doctoral researcher who had had the idea.

This example illustrates a range of collaborative, respectful and trusting relationships, for example, those between the researchers themselves as a team; the academic staff and doctoral researchers; the undergraduates and the doctoral researchers; and the museum working with the institution via the doctoral researchers. The example also raises matters related to professional conduct (discussed in Chapter 3). In organising this event, several issues needed to be addressed such as possible risks, including the potential for reputational harm to a prestigious museum or to the institution itself caused by upsetting families.

Another way to develop your track record as an effective communicator is to engage with undergraduates. What makes higher education an enjoyable experience for undergraduates is having teachers who are enthusiastic about the subjects they are teaching. As researchers are famed for their passion and enthusiasm for research, engaging with students is a ready-made match. Undergraduates will be curious to know about your research, especially as you are at the cutting-edge of knowledge in your discipline. As Information Box 2.2 indicates, there are many ways of engaging with undergraduates. There are also numerous ways to collaborating with them to create engagement activities for others, which will be of especial interest to those who wish to undertake public engagement work; we will discuss this again in Chapters 5 and 6 where we consider ways of engaging and the benefits of this activity, respectively.

Your peers

Threaded throughout the preceding sections is the notion of collaborating and engaging with your peers. Indeed, this is something that researchers usually do and are enthusiastic about, and it is impossible for us to exaggerate the value of such activity. The opportunities for learning from, and working with, your international colleagues and those in other disciplines will position you for future roles, which may not only be exclusively in academia. Most roles will require you to be able to work with a diverse range of other individuals and to cross boundaries; in other words, to be interdisciplinary or **inter-sectoral**.

If you and your peers can create a space or event for others to explore a topic and share their thoughts, you will be acting as exemplars to your researcher community as well as developing your skill-set through each other. We invite you to reflect on potential ways of engaging and/or collaborating with your peers by doing Activity 2.2.

Activity 2.2

Turning peers into potential collaborators

Make a list of all the researchers you know and their research areas within your institution. Are the people on the list mostly in your department and Faculty or do you know people across the institution? Do you know people from a variety of research interests or are they concentrated in one subject area?

Reflecting on this list further:

1. What does this tell you about your network within your institution?
2. Are there people or areas you would like, or need, to cultivate a connection with?
3. Is there a collaborative project you would like to explore with any of these people?
4. If so, what is the next step you should take to engage them further?

Managing your small steps

Smaller collaborations and engagement projects can be a most effective use of a busy researcher's time. As a doctoral researcher with a limited time frame to complete or an early-career researcher on a fixed-term contract, you may find you can achieve more on the shorter time-scales of smaller projects. Taking strategic decisions, such as what to do and when, is a simple way to manage your small steps into collaboration and engagement.

Once you begin to establish connections within your university and discipline, this can be expanded to inviting peer researchers from other institutions to come and talk, perhaps over coffee and buns, about current developments in your discipline. It is out of smaller discussions and interactions like these that bigger ideas come. A one-day conference, for instance, can be an excellent next step for postdoctoral researchers to begin collaborating with each other. By creating a platform for researchers to discuss and share their projects, engage with one another and develop new and interesting ideas, you will be demonstrating leadership skills.

Beginning to work with others

Working with others, especially those who may not thoroughly understand your specific research project or subject area, is not without challenges. One of the fundamental issues in collaborating and engaging with others is to ensure that everyone understands everyone else's position and viewpoint, and interdisciplinary collaborations and public engagement will bring this into sharp relief. The best advice is to never make assumptions about anything. The easiest and most common mistake to make is to assume you know what someone else means even if they use the same term. For instance, the notion of introversion is likely to mean something very different to a psychologist, mental health specialist and a researcher developer, while the concept of culture has different meanings even between anthropologists, depending on whether one is a social or cultural, British or American anthropologist, for example. Further, the term sustainability has multi-disciplinary use and meaning and, depending on the context, can be ambiguous.

Academia is full of potential conceptual variation and different understandings even before a group of people with diverse backgrounds come together to work on a common project. These variations will need to be explicitly identified and recognised. In Chapter 9 we suggest some activities you can use that will facilitate these kinds of discussion that an embryonic collaboration will need. However, starting out within your immediate research environment in terms of collaboration and engagement allows you to develop both experience and techniques for working with a diverse range of viewpoints and understanding.

As higher education is an international and diverse community, there will be plenty of opportunities for you to hone your skills in these areas. Indeed, we would encourage you to actively engage with people who are very different from yourself, especially those in contrasting disciplines. Again, as research problems are increasingly being addressed by interdisciplinary teams, the greater your exposure is to these issues early in your career, the better prepared you will be to meet those challenges when you are leading your own research project or interdisciplinary team. Our message, then, is to practise and explore, to be curious and creative.

When you begin to form your ideas for an event or activity, say a seminar, you may need to persuade people of its value and solicit their help to realise it.

Be prepared, though, for the idea to start evolving as soon as you begin sharing and engaging with others. We are now truly entering collaborative territory. For these conversations to be as successful and efficient as possible, you need to have a clear set of goals or objectives. Our advice is to list them before you meet others and discuss with a critical friend beforehand to ensure that what you wish to discuss is clear. To help you to focus on your idea for a collaboration, you could also create a concept map or mind-map, which we explain in Information Box 2.3. Effective collaborations are built upon successful connections and networks of trust (discussed by Erin Henslee in Chapter 8).

One important point about collaborative work to be mindful of is this: in any collaboration, you cannot force those that do not seem to be working with you to do things they do not want to do, nor can you make everyone agree with you. A collaboration is precisely what the word implies: co-labour – a working together. For this to be effective, productive and, importantly, as positive an experience as possible, every member of the collaborative group needs to be flexible, candid and willing to learn from each other.

Information Box 2.3

What is a concept map?

Concept maps are a graphical tool for organising and linking ideas. They have been shown to be useful in communicating ideas across disciplines (Heemskerk et al., 2003). For an overview of how to construct a concept map see Novak and Cañas (2006). There are also free downloadable online tools from CmapTools and MindMeister.

There are several methods you and your team can use to establish what people think and would like to do as part of the collaboration – and they all require mutual respect and some serious listening! Potential collaborators need to have compassion for each other and to be committed to the venture, as we discussed in Chapter 1. The best forms of collaboration and engagement will spend considerable time establishing what everyone means and what the objectives are, and how the team (even if it is a small one) will work together. Some larger projects can take as long as a year to work this out to ensure everyone is thinking in the same direction.

Once you and your collaborating or engaging team are under way, you will need to regularly review and 'check-in' or 'touch-base' with each other. The team will need to adopt a monitoring system to confirm if anything has changed, and that everyone's expectations and goals remain aligned. It is far better to be professional, play safe and even be pedestrian about this by using checklists and project management techniques, than to simply focus on the excitement of the collaboration or outcome, only to find yourself seen as being irresponsible and reckless. Top Tips 2.2 provides advice that was originally to help introverts, but it will be useful for all researchers who collaborate.

Top Tips 2.2

Not just for introverts; tips for everyone who collaborates

1. **When you can, plan.** If you are leading a group, you should ensure that you send agendas prior to meetings. This gives you time to prepare. You should include in the agenda the points you wish to get across, questions you have and any project debriefs you have scoped. Doing this preplanning helps to keep to a minimum the amount of context switching you need to do.

2. **Get it in the diary.** Put regular meetings into everyone's diaries from the outset if possible. This will form the basis of your monitoring and evaluation system. If meetings are held at the same time, every month, they will quickly become an established way of conducting business.

3. **Look out for opportunities.** Often the most innovative ideas come from spontaneous conversations, but these types of interaction can be draining, particularly if you are an introvert by nature. While these cannot (and should not) be avoided, the best way to be proactive about this is to try to spot opportunities early to enable you to plan.

4. **Practice.** Before a meeting, write down the two or three potential points you wish to get across, and then set yourself the target of conveying at least one of those when you are in the meeting. If you are new to collaborating, you are likely to find the need to practise the art of conveying all the points you intend; the more your practise, the more efficiently you will be able to get all points across in the time allocated for the meeting.

5. **Listen.** Everyone should listen very carefully to what is said and repeat back what is heard to clarify understanding. Additionally, all points discussed in the meeting should be confirmed with everyone.

Collaborative project management

One of the advantages of starting small in your institution is that the management of these projects is simplified by geographical proximity. Collaborating is, arguably, easier to initiate when you share a common infrastructure and internal working knowledge. This is not to say that these projects are simple; rather, that setting up a face-to-face meeting is more likely and easier to manage on a shared institutional calendar system. One of the things we have learned from collaborating across wider geographic space is that agreeing which software and platforms the team will use and how to share information is critical. The greater the distance between team members, the clearer everyone needs to be because the challenges of different time zones and varying access to the internet will force you to adjust your expectations and how you manage your usual work schedule. In short, allow far more time for everything than you would normally anticipate.

However, one of the advantages of differing times zones is that you can pass collaborative work, such as an article or chapter, around like a baton in a relay race! While one person or team is finishing for the day, the work can continue elsewhere in the world. We have used that advantage to write this book.

Another benefit to starting small is that learning to use project management frameworks and tools, such as Scrum/Agile or Trello, on a small project will be advantageous when you move on to a larger collaboration. Similarly, team-sharing software such as Google drive, Google docs, Doodle, Slack, MS Teams, is evolving rapidly; therefore, it would be advantageous to learn about this software early on in your career and in a comfortable environment. Trying to manage this in a new role or institution might be challenging.

In view of the variety of options at your disposal, all with their advantages and disadvantages, choosing between them is not a trivial task. We recommend discussing this with your university IT department or the department that handles technology for the classroom to see what systems they support. It is also important to discuss this with your collaboration team to determine if there are preferences or skills you can leverage in your decision making. Top Tips 2.3 has advice on project management software.

Top Tips 2.3

Project management software

We have taken the advice given on a blog post by Software Sustainability Institute (www.software.ac.uk/about), which suggests five key considerations when choosing collaborative software, and then adapted them for general researcher consideration:

1. **Documentation**. How will your collaborative team handle document-sharing and editing? If working internally, you may have existing file management systems in place, but you might want to consider how you collaborate in the future and outside

your institution. Systems like Dropbox, OneDrive, Google Drive, and so on may be more suitable for wider networks. However, first consider any data restrictions and security issues.

2. **Data restrictions and security**. Departments, schools or institutes may have pre-existing data storage and management rules, for example, prohibiting data storage on cloud platforms. The sensitivity of the data may also prohibit the use of some tools that could be deemed insecure. If you are unsure about the rules for your own department, first check with your supervisor or PI. You could also check with your university's dedicated data-management team.

3. **Community**. Familiarity with a specific tool can help efficiency, allowing your team to spend time on other tasks important to the project. However, even if you or a member of your team are familiar with something, you will need to consider the level of familiarity of other members of the team to ensure that the tool is usable for all parties.

4. **Perceived level of difficulty**. Usability of software is important, and your familiarity with a tool may bias you to the perceived difficulty of use. Be sure all members of your team are comfortable with learning the new tool and set some time aside for knowledge sharing so that those familiar can help those who may not be.

5. **Time availability**. You or your team might not have the amount of time required to set up and persuade everybody of the merits of using a specific tool, especially if you must launch the collaboration quickly to meet a time target (such as a proposal deadline). However, if you are planning a longer project, take your time and choose carefully. With all these tools available, once you pick one and invest in time to learn it, it is best to stay with it, so that the time invested is not wasted.

Avoiding commitment fatigue

There is always the possibility you will find new information or another opportunity as you continue to connect with others. You might be so excited by the range of opportunities you discover that it feels overwhelming. In our experience, people often stall at this point because either they are waiting to collect *all* the information they can, or they simply do not know what to agree to do. Common questions include: 'How do I manage this on top of the research I am already doing for my degree?' or 'How do I justify time away from my grant to work on this?' By starting small and committing to manageable activity, you will avoid overcommitting yourself and escape another reason for stalling – opportunity fatigue.

The checklist in Information Box 2.4 may help you to decide between activities and people. Prioritising your workload and interests will help to develop your strategic response, enabling you to become efficient in what you select to do.

Information Box 2.4

Checklist for filtering potential opportunities

Here is a list of questions to ask about opportunities that may present themselves. These will help you to prioritise and filter those that come your way (modified from Vitae's 'The Collaborative Researcher' workshop):

- Am I interested in this work?
- Will this move my research forward?
- Are there clear advantages to my career?
- What are the time constraints (how long will the project last)?
- Does the project have clear objectives and deadlines? Can I realistically meet them?
- Will I be motivated to do the work amidst my other commitments?
- Do I trust the people I will be working with?
- Is my role clear?
- Is there a clear and equitable strategy for sharing credit?
- Is my supervisor or PI supportive of this project?

If the answer is 'no', or 'I don't know' to any of these, seek clarification.

Internal opportunities may well lead to the creation of further opportunities, if, of course, you are open to such opportunities. Key characteristics that facilitate being open to new opportunity include being curious, brave and proactive. Do not be afraid to approach people, to ask them questions or to try out new strategies, ideas or experiments, and so on. This willingness to experiment should, after all, be innate to researchers, who experiment and play with ideas daily.

Now you have an insight into the opportunities for collaborating and engaging internally, it is time to venture outside your institution, exploring how you can engage externally, which we discuss in the next chapter.

Further reading

Heemskerk, M., Wilson, K. and Pavao-Zuckerman, M. (2003) Conceptual models as tools for communication across disciplines. *Ecology and Society*, 7(3), Art. 8.

Novak, J.D. and Cañas, A.J. (2006) The origins of the concept mapping tool and the continuing evolution of the tool. *Information Visualization*, 5(3): 175–184.

Simmons, N. and Singh, A. (2019) *Critical Collaborative Communities: Academic Writing Partnerships, Groups, and Retreats*. The Netherlands: Brill.

van Besouw, R.M., Rogers, K.S., Powles, C.J., Papadopoulos, T. and Ku, E.M. (2013) Organising, providing and evaluating technical training for early career researchers: a case study. *Innovations in Education and Teaching International*, 50(2): 1–11.

Vitae (n.d.) *Vitae: The Collaborative Researcher Workshop.* www.vitae.ac.uk/vitae-publications/vitae-library-of-resources/about-vitae-researcher-development-programmes/ (last date accessed 13/05/19).

3

How can doctoral and postdoctoral researchers engage externally?

In this chapter we invite you to consider:

- The variety of external organisations and sectors you could connect with
- The importance of maintaining professional conduct and of research integrity
- The differences between the cultures of academia and industry
- Some of the key benefits to doctoral, postdoctoral researchers and their institutions

The possibilities for external engagement are considerable; they provide doctoral and postdoctoral researches with a wide range of exciting opportunities to engage with industry, business, charities and policy makers. Entering these areas may not be easy or obvious for researchers; fortunately, institutions are increasingly facilitating this activity with programmes, training and schemes. Although there will be institutional leadership and protocols to follow, there is also room for individual creativity and ideas. This chapter will explore some of the common ways in which researchers can engage with people and organisations external to their own institution.

What kind of external engagement is possible?

As with internal engagement and collaboration, which we discussed in Chapter 2, one of the great features of universities is that they are full of the most incredible opportunities, assuming, of course, that you wish to get involved with collaborative and engagement work and that you know where to look for it and what to look for. If you are interested in such work, you will need to remain alert to the new possibilities because this is an area of rapid expansion and growth for universities with new possibilities emerging constantly. We have seen a growth of activity across disciplines too. Whereas a decade or so ago, external engagement was dominated by STEMM academics, now humanities, arts and social science (HASS) colleagues are forming relationships with a wide range of organisations too.

Here we consider some of the popular ways in which doctoral and postdoctoral researchers can engage externally with organisations beyond academia. While this is not an exhaustive list, we hope that it will stimulate your thinking about what you can do with your research knowledge. The only limitations will be your imagination, your time and any legal, ethical or health and safety requirements that you must consider. If you can think of creative ways in which you can use your research knowledge and expertise and can find the time to invest in exploring them, then you will find many exciting channels for external engagement.

Working with others in the spirit of cooperation is integral to collaboration, as we defined it in Chapter 1. It is often from such initial steps and forms of activity that more intense relationships can be formed. If you remain within academia, those relationships can frequently lead to longer-term partnerships. Indeed, cultivating external connections is increasingly becoming a part of normal academic life. Even if your career plans lie outside academia, this external experience can only enhance your CV.

Of course, successful collaboration and engagement require a certain mindset: one that is curious, creative and comfortable with the serendipitous outcomes that the uncertainty of encountering new experiences entails. Information Box 3.1 uses a fishing analogy to illustrate this point.

Information Box 3.1

Fishing for business

A fishing analogy for business collaboration from Stefanie Thorne, Director of Business Engagement and Entrepreneurship at the University of Suffolk:

- You never know what you are going to catch.
- Your failures will teach you as much as your successes.
- No two fishing expeditions are the same.
- You must put your fly out there to see what happens.
- Fight isn't won with first bite of the hook*.

(Continued)

- Many fish will be slippery and try to get away.
- Fishing puts us all out on the river together!

(Printed with kind permission.)

*Authors' note: Seldom is the fish won in the first encounter.

In the following sections we explore some of the common areas of activity (ponds to fish in) to illustrate the variety of ways researchers find to engage with external organisations. We will indicate different roles for doctoral and postdoctoral researchers, and highlight disciplinary differences, while providing practical help and advice.

Engaging with industry

As funders and government expect more economic impact for research investment, the landscape of collaboration with industry is becoming more commonplace. Many university and department websites proclaim their work with industry. It is common now for them to work with 'end-users' or the people who will benefit and apply the research. Many will have a strong track record of partnering with a specific industry or sector, such as aerospace, or the pharmaceutical or electronics sectors. These connections will be of considerable benefit if you are in those institutions and, better still, departments with close links to an industry or sector. We discuss in detail in Chapter 7 a UK scheme, that of Knowledge Transfer Partnerships (KTPs). If you are fortunate to be in such a department, it is highly likely that you will be exposed to industrial partners and the interactions they have with the university. Your doctoral research may be funded by industry: some companies provide doctorates in partnership with universities, for instance Hitachi and the University of Cambridge. Others provide placements in association within established programmes, such as with **research councils**' Cooperative Awards in Science and Engineering (or CASE) studentship scheme. There are also international opportunities, such as in European Horizon 2020 funded projects where external partners are required.

There are many schemes available, but sometimes it may simply be that your supervisor or PI has an industry or business connection that you can benefit from even if only to visit to gain an insight into what they do. Conversely, you can arrange for business/professional or industry contacts to visit your institution to see what you do. Indeed, inviting such people to give a talk to your department is a good way of starting to build external relationships and to extend your network. This is something we would especially encourage postdoctoral researchers to do. You may find your department is keen on this but does not have the staff resource to do so. The careers service, or research management and innovation services team if your institution has this, may also be able to suggest local businesses and supply contact information if you need help with identifying organisations or people to reach out to. Our Voice of Experience 3.1 provides an example of how external engagement with industry can benefit researchers.

Voice of Experience 3.1

Real-life career and consultancy advice

The South East Physics Network (SEPnet) held intensive training workshops for doctoral researchers in the region. These included a week-long Summer School that always consisted of people from industry who gave talks and provided insights into what their company or industry did.

One of the highlights of the week was an experiential workshop, The Consultancy Challenge. We approached companies that employed physics doctorates and invited them to provide us with real-life problems and challenges that their business or company was facing. These could be science-based or business-based and approximately 4–5 companies were involved, each with their own unique challenges for the doctoral researchers to address.

The participants worked in small teams to propose an approach to solving the problem. Usually, three to four teams worked separately on each problem. They needed to present this in two ways: first, in the form a short 'sales-pitch', and second, as a team poster. Representatives of the companies were available at various times during the Summer School to explain the company context, to answer questions and to act as judges for various awards: the best approach for each problem, the most effective pitch and the most eye-catching and interesting posters. We did have some companies who pursued this further, adopting the winning approach, and some participants were offered jobs, or at least interviews as a result of contact with a company at this event, when they completed their doctorates.

Here is a feedback quotation (anonymised) from a company representative:

> It was an absolute pleasure to be involved with the Summer School last week. It was very evident that all the participants had put in a massive amount of thought and effort to their case study. I have taken some great ideas away with me and will be doing a write-up on the day. I do intend to use some of the ideas that the students generated but maybe slightly adapted, and I shall let you know as and when this happens. Deciding a winner was very difficult as they all had great ideas.

(Continued)

The benefits of this encounter and exercise were many-layered. Participants needed to work together as a team, work on problems, and prepare pitches and posters. They were given real problems, which they appreciated, and they received feedback directly from 'the client'. The enthusiasm and excitement this activity created was amazing. Importantly, the researchers and the companies went away from the Summer School with a better appreciation of how collaboration between sectors can work.

I would say to researchers, researcher developers, supervisors and PIs – approach companies and ask if they have a real challenge that you could work on in the department or university. The impact on the professional development of researchers can be immense and you may have established a new external relationship too.

Dr Dawn Duke – designer of The Consultancy Challenge

If you would like to make contacts or simply find out what is happening outside academia, look out for industry open days or fairs for industry in your local area. There will also be subject-specific or sector-focused events held at all levels: regional, national and international. All professions have these. For example, boat, car, gardening, gaming and technology shows will furnish you with a glimpse into what is trending in those areas. You may be able to see potential connections or make a contact at such events – at a minimum, you will have enjoyed a day out looking at the world from a different perspective. Moreover, these kinds of event are open to a wide audience and tend not to be targeted exclusively at scientists and engineers.

All large organisations, irrespective of industry, have a range of internal functions and services, such as estates, finance, human resources, marketing, and so on, that may welcome collaboration with a cutting-edge researcher like you. There is a tendency for researchers in HASS areas to dismiss STEMM-based industries too quickly, erroneously assuming that they have nothing to offer in a science-based context. However, all industries employ and work with and for people, for example, using artistic and social input to improve working environments, relationships and products and create advertising, exhibitions and archives. Thus, the skills and knowledge developed in HASS have widespread applications.

Engaging with NGOs and charities

One of the most likely sources of engagement is with charities and non-government organisations (NGOs). Many charities are the 'end-users' of research and play a large role as sources for public engagement with research. From human health issues to local historical associations, they provide ample opportunity for researchers who wish to engage with the public and community. We explore this area in more detail in Chapters 5 and 6.

While NGOs are normally unaffiliated with academia, there is a strong desire across the academy to form partnerships with them to produce real impact from research. Duncan Green, Senior Strategic Adviser at Oxfam GB, has written many articles on why he, and others in the sector, believe this partnership does not occur as frequently as it should. Barriers include crucial aspects such as timelines, competing pressures and underlying motivations. NGOs, for example, since they must react to a given circumstance, have a much greater sense of urgency than researchers in academia.

Nevertheless, there remains great potential for engagement. For instance, local SMEs (small and medium-sized enterprises) may welcome your expert advice or knowledge, so you could provide free consultancy or even practical help, such as setting up a website. No matter what your subject, local or national interest groups and societies could be approached either with an offer to give a talk about your research or to see if they would like to collaborate to develop a project idea. Many have boards of governance where your specialist input would be very helpful; for instance, housing associations might be looking for civil engineers, housing policy researchers, urban landscape researchers, and so on. Researchers are often welcome to the Women's Institute or similar social groups to give a talk or to discuss prevalent social issues.

One major area for NGOs is fundraising. This is an opportunity for you to think creatively on how you could partner with the NGO towards their fundraising goals. For example, could you provide a talk at an annual event? Could you host your own thematic event at your institution or in your local community? Universities can often be a great resource for NGOs in terms of access to expertise, hosting events, creating student groups, and embedding in local communities. Look for ways to leverage not only your skills and expertise but also your wider institution.

Engaging with policy makers

Academics tend to wait until their research is completed before they contact policy makers, believing that only then do they have something of interest to say. While not wrong, it does leave things rather late – certainly in the fast-moving world of politics, in which topics of interest arise and then are rapidly replaced by another. However, many national politicians as well as local government officials and politicians have enduring interests and will often welcome free advice. You can begin on a smaller scale by engaging with councils and local government officials, then consider any national placement schemes that may be available (the UK has such a scheme). Your institution may have individuals or a unit that specialises in engaging with policy makers and who will certainly be able to help and advise you on how to approach officials and policy makers; they may offer training as well. With all policy makers and politicians, it is best to contact them to let them know what you are working on and, with the support of your supervisor or PI of course, you can offer, then, to keep them informed or 'briefed' on the subject.

This is an area where postdoctoral researchers can play a leading role – by researching or finding out who has an interest in your subject area, or where you and your PI might be able to provide advice and influence outcomes. You probably should not expect to lead on this, but rather prepare the ground for the PI and politicians to meet. However, you can gain experience of preparing briefing notes and papers, making contact, arranging meetings, setting the scene, writing press releases. Do not underestimate how valuable all this is for things to run smoothly and professionally. While you are working behind the scenes or in the service of your PI, you can be sure that policy makers, politicians and CEOs will all have people working behind the scenes doing similar activities – these are valuable contacts to network with as you simultaneously develop your respective careers. You will then both have a well-established relationship and connections to draw on when you fill more powerful positions.

Engaging with social enterprise

It is often said that what draws people to research and academia is that they want to make a difference and to change the world for the better, even if in just a small way. Social enterprises and not-for-profit organisations have a good deal of appeal in this respect, frequently providing a way for the social sciences, arts and humanities to engage externally to contribute to broader society.

In terms of training, development and researcher engagement, in universities this is a more recent area of activity than the usual business enterprise. There may not be the volume of equivalent opportunities that exist around the commercialisation of research, for instance, but once you begin to make enquiries, you will probably find more than you expect. A good place to start is by identifying who is working in this area within your own or neighbouring institutions. One of the most inspiring examples of social enterprise for researchers is Ketso®, the story of which we provide in Information Box 3.2.

Information Box 3.2

Ketso® – a social spin-out

Many universities provide resources to support Spin-Out companies formed to commercialise products manufactured or created as a result of research. It is a commonly held misconception that Spin-Outs must be technology based. Although many are, this is by no means true of all.

Ketso® (whose use we describe in Chapter 9) was set up to further a social mission by Dr Joanne Tippett at The University of Manchester. The fact that Ketso is not based on technology makes it interesting. It sells a hands-on, ethical product. The kit was designed to make lessons around effective engagement with stakeholders, learned in Joanne's ESRC-funded (Economic and Social Research Council) PhD and postdoctoral fellowships, available to a wider audience.

While working in rural regeneration in Lesotho, Joanne found that women were less likely to have a say in mixed gender groups. She created a **pedagogy** that ensured everyone was able to contribute and have their ideas captured. In the 10 years since turning these ideas into a portable kit, Ketso has been used in 68 countries with over 25,000 participants.

See https://ketso.com/ for more information.

Do not eschew, then, the commercial or business training that universities provide. While many universities have 'incubator' schemes for budding entrepreneurs, you do not need to have a ready-made business idea to benefit from their knowledge and experience. Many of these schemes offer training and advice that you can use simply to explore the potential and possibilities of your research. Indeed, all organisations and the people who work in and for them need business and financial acumen and to understand production and employment matters to some degree.

There are so many options in this area that, even if you never have an idea that you can turn into a product or service or do not become a social entrepreneur yourself, by simply observing, considering and being involved in an existing external engagement, you will learn more than you may realise. Activity 3.1 may provide you with some ideas based on our discussion so far.

Activity 3.1

What could you do?

Having read our examples and advice, think about which industries, businesses or NGOs, etc., you could approach locally or nationally, with an aspect of your research. What aspects might interest them? Try to find something for each sector, no matter how outrageous the

(Continued)

idea. By imagining, we create a mental picture of how the future could be, and this might result in something to act on when you are motivated and inspired to do so.

Sector	What aspect of your research might they be interested in? Alternatively, what expert knowledge could you offer to each sector? What would you like in return?	Who would you need to contact? Think of a specific role or head of department.
Natural resources and the environmental sector, including agriculture, fishing, wind power, mining – often called the Primary sector		
Industrial or Secondary sector, including manufacturing, engineering, construction		
Creative and culture industries, including artists, museums, film and gaming		
Charity, non-governmental organisation (NGO)		
Services or Tertiary sector, including tourism, restaurants, financial and professional services, including health and social services		
Knowledge or Quaternary sector, including intellectual, education, research		
Policy and high-level decision making (government, industry), sometimes called the Quinary sector		

Going global

There are schemes and programmes that encourage researchers to experience work and life in other countries. The Worldwide Universities Network (WUN) is well known for the international exchanges and interaction it provides. Similarly, there are programmes encouraging mobility across the European Research Area. These are all excellent initiatives, and you may have access to more within your own country. However, not everyone is able to benefit from them. For many researchers, going global might begin, oddly enough, within your own department and institution.

One of your authors once observed a university careers event where several employers mentioned that they were looking for people with team-working skills, business acumen, international understanding and the ability to work in an international setting. A student participant commented at the end that there was no opportunity to develop an international understanding. However, there were several different nationalities and international students and researchers in the room. Your international colleagues are a source of information and insight while later, as alumni, they become potential collaborators.

A key area of global engagement occurs via academic conferences. This can be both in terms of travelling to an international conference (and we hope that doctoral researchers have at least one of these) and by meeting international delegates. Another way is to collaborate with colleagues to organise your own. Pam Denicolo, in Voice of Experience 3.2, offers useful advice for you to do so.

Voice of Experience 3.2

Organising conferences with international colleagues

Being on the Executive Committees of international associations, one in psychology and one in education, has afforded me opportunities to organise conferences in many distant lands with colleagues resident there. As well as being successful and great fun, they have all provided cultural learning experiences about collaboration across borders beyond the eponymous discipline.

Always remember to be precise. The advent of more rapid communication channels has helped avoid cultural near disasters (depending on your perspective). I recall one such near disaster: having sent a quick affirmative answer to the question in an email about whether alcohol could be served at the conference dinner, we were met on every table with a huge flagon, each with a tap/faucet, of vodka, but no wine. Now I will always check on the local customs for celebratory meals.

Discuss details and assumptions about important aspects. The photographs of the ancient mid-European seminary that was suggested as the accommodation venue showed a charming historical residence. Participants, having flown across the globe before being bused up a mountain, arrived late at night to find each truckle-bed had all its linen neatly folded at its foot, ready for making up, and a towel, as specified in the brochure, except that it was the size of handkerchiefs – rather inadequate for some of us larger folk. On another occasion, the U.S. 'Ladies Private School' that provided accommodation for our mixed-gender meeting had boasted that it had, in 10 study-bedroom blocks, 'showers' and 'washing basins' for each person. It was a surprise to find that these facilities were not, as assumed, 'en suite'. Instead, all occupied one room, five showers down each side, opening out onto two rows of basins facing each other down the centre. That called for the immediate purchase of even larger towels and diplomatic gaze-averting as folk exited showers. Domestic issues are as important as the conference presentation programme.

(Continued)

Joining in with the spirit of things is a way to build networks and remain friends. Two learning experiences from international conferences in Scandinavia stand out in my mind in addition to the wonderful hospitality. One was joining forces and making the best of things with others from poorer countries (in which 'university credit cards' did not exist) by sharing pizza and coke dinners because of the high cost of restaurant food. The conference fee had been reasonable, but it did not include meals other than the final dinner. The other was at the conference dinner, when we were all sat at our 'national tables'. After the food, each Scandinavian group provided a resounding song from their home country. We could do nothing but put aside our national reserve to provide a rendition of our own, which produced a great cheer. Information about the cost of living of the venue is useful in advance – but some unexpected cultural customs can make you surprise yourself.

Watch your language. Assuming a common language can bring surprises too. After presenting a keynote paper in Australia, I was invited by some of the men in the audience to 'put on my thongs' to join them on the beach later. Thank goodness I realised that they meant what I called 'flipflops' and not the scanty underwear that are called thongs in the UK.

Pam Denicolo – Emeritus Professor

What especially needs to be considered when working externally?

Getting involved with an external collaboration and engagement is not something you can just do alone. Even researchers who have 'gone under the radar' (see Chapter 10) have done so within the support of the university environment. Their supervisors and PIs may not have been aware of their activity, but someone in the institution was. This is important because there are some aspects of working externally that need to be both considered and taken seriously, not least of which is your personal safety and well-being. At a minimum, someone should know where you are and what you are doing, just as we would expect when conducting fieldwork, say, in research.

Professional conduct, research integrity and personal safety

For collaborative and engagement activity to be successful, it needs to be conducted in a professional way, no matter how enthusiastic the researcher. There will always be wider issues and sensitivities to consider, some of which we will discuss again when we explore networks of trust and resistance in Part III.

The Universities UK's Concordat on Research Integrity was drawn up recognising that: 'All those engaged with research have a duty to consider how the work they undertake, host or support impacts on the research community and on wider society.' (See Further Reading below.)

Reflection Point 3.1

Professional values

Take a moment to reflect on your professional values. What are they, and what matters to you? Check any values declared by your discipline or professional society and consider how your values marry up with them.

If you want to engage externally, you should do so through your institution, department or discipline. There are areas of risk or concern that, as a research professional, will be integral to your vocation. In Chapter 8 we have a checklist of areas that will require a contract or written agreement, including authorship and data management, among other points, that could otherwise be contentious (see Information Box 8.1). Here we simply indicate general areas of concern through Activity 3.2, which may help you to identify those areas you need to consider further.

Activity 3.2

Thinking about engaging externally

When thinking about engaging externally or getting involved with an activity, even if it is supported by your institution, consider the following questions:

- Are there likely to be products or outcomes that raise intellectual property questions?
- Are there likely to be any legal implications concerning this engagement?
- Are there likely to be any commercial property concerns affecting this engagement?
- Are there any ethical issues I should be concerned about?
- Are there any environmental issues I should be concerned about?
- Are there any procurement issues that will affect this engagement?
- Are there any open-data issues that will affect this engagement?
- Am I aware of the above issues, and do I know where to get advice?

If your answer to this last question is 'no', seek out the following people or departments in your institution (your institution may not have all these offices, but someone should be able to provide advice on these matters):

(Continued)

- Personal safety office or regulations
- Research integrity or governance officers
- Those responsible for ethical approvals
- Health and safety officers
- Environmental or sustainability officers
- Procurement and/or finance officers
- Research data management office (often the Library)
- Social responsibility officers

Different working cultures and ethos

Clearly, the way academics and businesspeople operate, communicate with each other and view the world, is very different, but engaging with one another does not have to be frustrating. Being aware of potential differences early in the relationship is a good first step towards reducing the potential for frustrations to build. Indeed, it would be a good idea to spend some time, in the early stages, not only to get to know each other but also to discuss and agree how team members would like to work together and be treated. You and your colleagues on the project could draw up some team rules or a code of conduct. Agreeing these basic issues will be especially important when working with people and organisations that have different working cultures and ways of doing things. Information Box 3.3 offers a light-hearted insight into some of the cultural differences between academia and industry.

Information Box 3.3

What do they really want?

Academics want	Industry wants
Long-term research outcomes	Short-term deliverables/outputs
To give an hour-long presentation	To receive no more than a five-minute summary
Decisions that are achieved by committee	Decisions that are achieved by managers/leaders
To suggest that all ideas are equally valid – in theory – and the responsibility must lie with the author(s) cited	To ensure that ideas have clear ownership or sponsorship – the responsibility must lie with some line manager
To critique every angle and idea	To agree on one angle and idea (ideally right now!)
To write an 8,000-word paper – with lots of references and preferably involving complex diagrams and/or equations	To receive a 350-word report – with: • Executive summary • Bullet points • Accessible diagrams

Academics want	Industry wants
To explore the whole range of possibilities and arguments (or ideally to do more research on the subject)	Academics to cut to the point!
Esteem and acolytes	Money and more money
An impact assessment or case study with which to impress the funders	An impact assessment with return on investment attached with which to impress the CEO

Information Box 3.3, while perhaps somewhat exaggerated, does raise an issue that is much commented on by those involved in external engagement and collaboration: how different the culture or way of doing things are compared with university. Generally, researchers comment on the volume and quality of the meetings and almost always on the attitude towards time. One of our favourite observations, cited in Voice of Experience 3.3, is from a postdoctoral researcher who had been on an industrial placement scheme. It would be easy to underestimate the level and quality of different ways of working, but if you are following our Collaborative Code (see Chapter 1, Information Box 1.2), then you know that it is vital to enquire, to listen carefully to the other and to confirm understanding. We pick this topic up again in Chapter 10 where we discuss resistance.

Voice of Experience 3.3

They have 'drop-dead dead-lines'

I had an internship with a large international telecommunications company. I found the first few weeks very strange. The way my manager and the team worked was very different from my PI and research team and what I was used to. The company had team meetings every week, and the line manager wanted to see me every day. At first, I found that difficult and, to be honest, intrusive. I thought he was checking up on me. But after a few weeks, I realised that I was looking forward to the meetings. I enjoyed the way the company managed the work and the way everyone in the team contributed to the meetings. My line manager was genuinely interested in what I thought. I am not saying my PI was not interested, just that it felt different. I felt as if I was working with the line manager – as part of a team. I found it very supportive. It made me realise that I much preferred that kind of working. I would not have been aware of that if I hadn't been on the internship scheme. They offered me a job at the end of it. Although I turned it down because I wanted to finish my research, I know

(Continued)

that I will go back and work in industry when the research ends. I would thoroughly recommend taking up a placement if possible. I found it extremely useful to see how another organisation did things and enjoyable too.

One thing, though, that did come as a bit of a surprise, was the way they managed deadlines; they really were it! There was no extension – no compromise – nothing. It is not like that in academia. We are always shifting things around and extending deadlines. Another postdoc on the scheme had noticed this too and summed it up beautifully. He said: 'they have real deadlines; they have drop-dead dead-lines!'

Postdoctoral researcher – Electronics and engineering

Being mindful of the nuances and differences between academic practice and that of other kinds of organisation will be beneficial for your future work either within or beyond academia because differences in culture occur between universities too. As the higher education environment becomes more diverse, being sensitive to differences and being able to respond constructively to them is a skill that will become increasingly important in your career.

What are the wider benefits of external engagement?

The wider benefits to individual researchers, at all career levels, and to their supervisors, PIs and institutions of engaging externally are considerable, not only in terms of the range and variety of opportunity available, but also for the personal and professional benefit it has too. The wide range of opportunity does, we hope, reinforce the point we made in Chapter 1 that there should be value for everyone in these areas.

The benefits to researchers

For a researcher, encountering people from outside the discipline will broaden the scope and the way you think about your research. Being challenged by a member of the public or a five-year-old to explain what you are doing will force you to think in more depth about the nature of your research so that you can address the question in a readily understandable way to the person who asked it. For doctoral researchers, it may lead to ideas and resources that lead to a postdoctoral position or a role in another sector. Indeed, every aspect of collaborating and engaging is good for your career and CV. It will bring new contacts and networks to doctoral and postdoctoral researchers alike; some may be possible future employers or perhaps new friends. Illustrating the benefits of collaboration with industry, Voice of Experience 3.4 describes how one doctoral researcher took an idea for a teaching tool from concept to practice, developing his own new area research along the way.

Voice of Experience 3.4

From concept to kit to international collaboration

I was a second year PhD student in 2014 when I proposed the 'Design, Assemble and Dismantle (DAD)' Project to the Head of the Department (HoD). The HoD liked the idea and I, together with a friend in industry, designed the kit and his company produced the necessary design documents for manufacturing. It took the company a few months to produce the technical drawings, and I convinced the University Workshop to manufacture the kit. The outcome of the collaboration was the first full-scale teaching kit in our department, which has been used by both undergraduate and postgraduate students every year since 2015.

The establishment of this collaboration was quick because it was through my old friend in industry. In less than two months, my friend and I were working together on the design of the new kit. The Head of the Department and the Director of Undergraduate Studies were very supportive from the beginning. However, the Manager of the University Workshop believed that we should outsource the manufacturing.

Considering the high cost for the outsourcing, I spent a few months patiently convincing the workshop manager to manufacture the kit in house. Part of the resistance was due to this being the first time someone had asked the University Workshop to make a full-scale kit. A couple of years later, when I needed to manufacture the second kit, there was no resistance and everything was much smoother.

Later, I was chairing a session on 'teaching spatial structures' in a conference in Japan, and a Mexican lecturer presented a paper on design and construction of bamboo structures as an educational project. Following his presentation, I introduced him to the DAD Project and suggested to him to set up the collaboration. This happened in September 2016, and we organised the first exchange in early 2017. Parallel to this collaboration, I proposed a similar collaboration to one of my friends who is an Iranian lecturer. Here again, it took us a few months to set up the collaboration, and the first group of Iranian students exchanged their design with Surrey students in early 2017. Educational collaboration on the DAD Project was very successful, and two other universities from Brazil and China are going to join the collaboration next year.

I discussed this collaboration during my first job interview as a case study, and all the interview panel members were convinced this was a successful project. Also, I was recently awarded an international grant to develop another full-scale teaching kit.

Dr Alireza Behnejad, Teaching Fellow

We also see opportunities for developing leadership skills, which are important for all researchers, in collaborating and engaging. Balancing the demands of research alongside external engagement will enhance your management skills. Further, it provides a vehicle for trying out a different potential professional area while working on a research project for a funder or PI. In view of these benefits, we invite you, in Reflection Point 3.2, to consider which sector(s) would be especially beneficial for you to forge a collaboration with.

Reflection Point 3.2

What inspires you?

Based on the examples and suggestions you have encountered so far, which of the benefits we have outlined appeal to you most? In which area or sector might you consider collaboration or engagement to achieve that benefit?

Of course, you could start your own business, although that is a major commitment and requires considerable effort. While we would always encourage a budding entrepreneur, taking small initial steps, as we discussed in Chapter 2, would be wise. Smaller steps could include exploring what others have done, and are doing, with research in your subject area as well as investigating what your research and innovation service or office provide. There may be regional professional bodies or business associations or partnerships holding networking events that you could join. By being involved with external organisations you will gain an extraordinary insight into how they function and what they need, and thus will be able to work effectively in many worlds.

The benefits of external engagement to PIs, supervisors, senior managers and the institution

In many ways, the benefits to supervisors and PIs of external engagement are akin to appreciating a doctoral researcher's move towards independence. Further, external engagement brings new contacts and fresh ideas into the academy.

The potential to be leveraged by supervisors and PIs through their researchers is frequently under-used. An example of such potential is demonstrated by the ICURe programme, cited in Information Box 3.4. This programme will be of direct interest to PIs as it utilises early-career researchers to bridge the gap between their academic ideas and industry. The researcher acts on behalf of the research team to explore the commercial potential of their research. At the heart of this model is the notion that the researcher is a broker or explorer who ventures forth on behalf of busy academics. Such a model can be applied to all aspects of external engagement and be of interest to supervisors also.

Information Box 3.4

SET Squared and ICURe

SET Squared is a partnership between the Universities of Bath, Bristol, Exeter, Southampton and Surrey. It is a 'business incubator' that helps take ideas and turn them into thriving businesses. SET Squared has been highly successful. As their website says: 'Since launching in 2002, we have supported over 3,500 entrepreneurs helping them raise £1.8bn investment.' The number of 'spin-out' companies by students and staff, and the impact on the local economy, have been impressive. SET Squared provide training, advice and expertise to researchers at all stages of their career. For doctoral and postdoctoral researchers, they offer a *Researcher to Innovator* programme that helps them to turn innovative ideas into business propositions.

A recent initiative, the ICURe programme, *Innovation to Commercialisation of University Research*, is aimed at postdoctoral researchers. It enables them to explore the commercial potential of research. ICURe fellows receive training and funding to conduct market research. Specifically, they help to bridge the gap between research, innovation and commercialisation.

The entrepreneurial training and support offered by such organisations as SET Squared afford researchers the opportunity to take their research into (sometimes) unimagined territory. In their words: 'Some of the world's most disruptive technologies have originated from university research.'

See www.setsquared.co.uk/.

The reputational and financial benefits of external engagement are probably well established in institutions and within senior management teams. However, whether the contribution of doctoral and postdoctoral researchers is equally recognised is another matter. We often hear that doctoral researchers cost universities more than they bring in financially and that research is cost neutral (the same money in and out through Full Cost funding mechanisms). However, we suspect that the informal income and soft power that these researchers generate via external engagement provides a different cost/benefit story.

This brings Part I of this book to a close. We have set the scene and, hopefully, provided you with some insight into the general context in which doctoral and postdoctoral researchers can collaborate and engage with others. We hope, also, that you have found something in the preceding chapters to arouse your curiosity and lead you to further exploration within your institution and discipline, and beyond them too.

In Part II we will tease out some of these issues in more detail, drawing on the experiences and lessons learned from public engagement activity and models of doctoral training and knowledge exchange in the UK. It is clear to us that collaborative and engagement work can have, and indeed is having, an impact on the personal and professional development of researchers. We will explore this area in the next chapter, which opens Part II.

Further reading

Author Services (n.d.) *Getting Your Research into the UK Parliament.* A how-to guide from Taylor & Francis, Sense about Science and POST. Retrieved from: https://authorservices.taylorandfrancis.com/getting-your-research-into-parliament/

Fairchild, R. et al. (n.d.) *An Introductory Guide to Research/Industry Collaborations.* University of Bath. Retrieved from: www.bath.ac.uk/marketing/public-engagement/assets/Guide_to_engaging_with_industry_FINAL.pdf

Green, D. (2016) *How Change Happens.* Oxford: Oxford University Press

Maeda, J. (2009) Academia vs. industry: the difference is in the punctuation marks. *Harvard Business Review*, 24 March. Retrieved from: hbr.org/2009/03/academia-vs-industry-the-diffe

New Scientist (2012) Industrial PhDs: exploring the dark side. *New Scientist*, 15 February. Retrieved from: www.newscientist.com/article/mg21328522-700-industrial-phds-exploring-the-dark-side/

The Conversation (2016) Ten rules for successful research collaboration. *The Conversation*, 15 February. Retrieved from: http://theconversation.com/ten-rules-for-successful-research-collaboration-53826

Universities UK (n.d.) *The Concordat to Support Research Integrity.* Retrieved from: www.universitiesuk.ac.uk/policy-and-analysis/reports/Pages/research-concordat.aspx

World Intellectual Property Organisation (n.d.) *World Intellectual Property Organisation.* Retrieved from: www.wipo.int/about-ip/en/universities_research/ip_policies/faqs/index.html

PART II
Success is in the detail

4

What are the benefits of collaborating and engaging?

In this chapter you are invited to consider:

- The kinds of people who undertake collaborative and engagement work
- The key skills that doctoral and postdoctoral researchers can gain from being involved in this work
- What you might learn as a result of getting involved
- Some of the main personal and professional benefits for researchers

We also invite doctoral supervisors, Principal Investigators (PIs) and stakeholders to consider:

- Some of the benefits that might accrue to them
- How they can support and facilitate the benefits of involvement for researchers

In this chapter we apply a professional development approach to explore what researchers can learn from collaborating and engaging with others, and how personal and professional benefit can be leveraged from working in these areas. Clearly, there has been a wealth of collaborative activity, and inspiring examples of engagement abound; however, there is far more to be obtained from this activity, as we shall see.

What kind of people collaborate and engage?

In Chapter 1, we indicated that there is 'something for everyone' in collaborating and engaging with others, and that you are not required to be a certain personality type or indeed at a certain stage in your career or level of seniority.

All kinds of people can and do get involved in this work, and we continue to highlight this point. We emphasise that there are no right or wrong person- alities for engaging and collaborating with others, that is everyone (and we do mean everyone) can be involved in some way or another. This kind of activity takes you beyond your research and enables you to use your research in differ- ent ways, which, in turn, enhances the range of your experience.

Although collaborating and engaging do not require any specific *personal* attrib- utes, they do assume certain *professional* characteristics and a specific professional disposition. This means that unless you have been actively involved in this kind of work previously, it is quite likely that you will need to develop or acquire some new skills. The wonderful thing about collaborative working and engagement activity, though, is that they are the perfect vehicles for enhancing and enabling precisely the qualities and skills you need (see Activity 4.1).

We, the authors, firmly believe that there is much to be gained from collabo- rating and engaging if you can leverage the informal learning inherent in this kind of work, and that this is of considerable benefit to doctoral and postdoc- toral researchers alike. It will enable you to develop a range of professional skills that, in turn, can help you to position yourself for future roles, particularly those roles where demonstrating 'leadership' and an inclusive approach to team work- ing might be required. As we remarked in Chapter 1, collaborative working and engaging with others allow you to develop a proven 'track record', the evidence of your abilities that many employers, including academic ones, require. It is important, then, to be aware of the professional qualities or characteristics and skill-sets that are common attributes for those involved with this kind of activity.

Certainly, being self-aware, in respect of knowing and understanding your strengths and recognising and appreciating your positive traits, arguably is the most important professional attribute you can cultivate. This will also require you to be aware of those areas you need to improve on, are not so good at or are, perhaps, not the best aspects of one's personality (and we all have those). Self-awareness is not easy to acquire because it comes from reflecting and taking feedback from our peers, friends and colleagues, which can be uncomfortable at times; yet, this process should be constructive and help us change behaviour (and should never be personal or damaging). Self-awareness, then, is cultivated through **reflective practice**, or 'debriefing' yourself, if you prefer. It is through self-awareness that professionals can appraise themselves, assess their situation and make improvement.

Everyone agrees that collaborations and engagement can yield something that is greater in sum than the component parts. However, to achieve that, all contributors to the project/activity will need to work at it and be committed to the idea. There are, then, some principles that we believe researchers must adhere to irrespective of the nature of the collaboration/engagement, which we synthesised into the Collaborative Code discussed in Chapter 1. First, you must be committed to the relationship and act of collaborating, no matter at what level you are participating. There is much that can be learned, even if you are a junior member of a partnership established at higher levels. Truly collaborative projects and public engagement will, ideally, entail the attributes of co-design, co-production, cooperation, commitment, and perhaps even co-delivery and co-implementation.

If you are curious to know the extent to which you already have a disposition for collaborating and/or engaging, you might wish to do Activity 4.1.

Activity 4.1

Disposition checklist

Read the following list, and delete or circle your preference, as appropriate (there are no 'right or wrong' answers):

- Do you mostly prefer to work on your own? YES/NO
- Do you like to take calculated risks? YES/NO
- Do you find it easy to talk to family, friends and non-academics about your research? YES/NO
- Do you consider others when making decisions? YES/NO
- Would you sacrifice your best idea for the sake of the team? YES/NO
- Do you enjoy different situations and meeting different people? YES/NO
- When you do something new, do you reflect on your performance and the impact you have on those around you? YES/NO

If you answered YES to most of these questions, you may already have cultivated a disposition for collaborating, sharing and engaging. If you answered mostly NO, or half YES and half NO, you can cultivate a more open stance according to the activities you choose to do, or ensure the team include these in their work.

Merle Richards et al. (2001) identify caring human relationships as being at the heart of professional collaborative activity. This is Number 1 in our Collaborative Code – you will need to be, and be seen to be, compassionate and caring in a professional role. Good collaborators and engagers care about the welfare of the people involved as much as the research or project outcome. Richards et al. also say that it is important to establish rapport among partners and between the participants in order to create and develop mutual understanding. They advise that you should be sensitive to diverse cultures and aim to determine objectives, goals and outcomes in a democratic way. There is quite a range of attributes or characteristics inherent in this process, which, unless you stop to consider them closely, could easily pass by unnoticed.

At the initial level, there is the skill of talking to a range of people using your ability to match your message to their understanding, which, in turn, implies you have taken the time to get to know them and to appreciate their position. This requires all the skills involved in actively listening, especially checking that you have understood what people intended to convey, not just what you thought, assumed or imagined you heard. Collectively, these are communication skills, but there is far more to these than giving a presentation about your research. It suggests a fundamental, yet respectful, curiosity about others (Number 3 in our Collaborative Code). This need not be a natural personal trait; you simply should be aware that you will need to 'check-in' and ask questions in a professional capacity, to avoid making assumptions about others' perspectives. Richards et al. (2001) go on to suggest that this all requires an 'ethic of inquiry' and an 'ethic of action' that lead everyone to accept there is no single way of knowing and that everyone agrees to contribute something to the process. All of this implies a creative and constructivist approach (Numbers 5 and 6 in the Collaborative Code, respectively).

Ethics of inquiry and of action should become part of your essential stance, especially when working with other disciplines, communities and cultures. This will enable you to agree realistic expectations and establish a common language and set of goals. You can achieve this by being open and candid (Number 4 in our Collaborative Code) with each other and by agreeing that everyone is committed to the outcome (Number 2 in the Collaborative Code).

This may all seem a daunting prospect initially, but if you start small and develop the basic skills, by way of some of the opportunities we discussed in Chapter 2, you will gradually but definitely develop your abilities from there. This reinforces the point made at the beginning of this book (see Barnett, cited in Walsh and Kahn (2010), in Chapter 1) that you need a willingness to learn, change and grow. We are all capable of this no matter what our personality type is.

What key characteristics and skills are needed?

Initially, you will need to reflect on, and review, the range of your management skills. These will include time, project, financial and people management skills. You will not need to be the world's leading expert in these, but you should understand the basic principles and be alert to those aspects you may need to develop further.

Project management

All those working together on the project will need some level of project management skill because everyone will be contributing something tangible or a deliverable. The larger the collaboration/engagement activity, the more adaptable the management tools and the people will need to be. Therefore, a more flexible approach rather than a linear project management model might be preferable. Irrespective of the size of the project, you will need to plan a schedule of work. A **Gantt chart** is the most common method of planning and monitoring project progress (for an example, see Information Box 4.1).

Information Box 4.1

Sample schedule for collaborative project

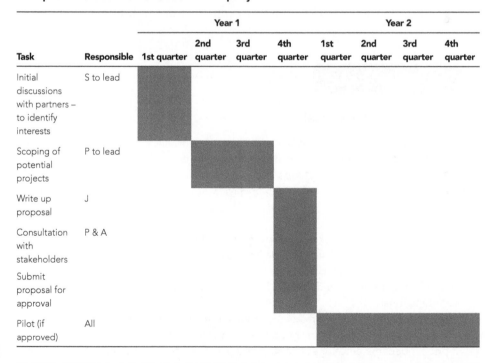

Task	Responsible	Year 1				Year 2			
		1st quarter	2nd quarter	3rd quarter	4th quarter	1st quarter	2nd quarter	3rd quarter	4th quarter
Initial discussions with partners – to identify interests	S to lead	██							
Scoping of potential projects	P to lead		██						
Write up proposal	J			██					
Consultation with stakeholders	P & A			██					
Submit proposal for approval				██					
Pilot (if approved)	All				██	██	██	██	██

Even if you are part of a larger project, you will still need to plan out your contribution in much the same way as you plan and project manage your own research. You should consider if the allocation of tasks is fair or needs to be realigned. It is important to determine who will ensure this is the case and who will keep the project on track, as well as who will keep everyone informed of what is happening. People may need to adopt more than one role. This is especially the case if the collaboration is a small one, say between two researchers, where each of you will need to ensure you have all the project management requirements covered. Therefore, you will also need to cultivate a proactive response, enquiring about whether things are progressing as they ought. This will require your monitoring and evaluation skills.

Difficult conversations

Research work and outcomes require transparency of process and accountability at all levels, especially if funding and/or human participants are involved. You may also find it useful to take training in holding 'difficult conversations' and in how to spot a 'false consensus', where it seems that people agree, but in fact they do not. We proffer some advice on how to approach this in Information Box 4.2.

Information Box 4.2

How to deliver bad news well

Both giving and receiving bad news is hard, so prepare well. It is a good idea to write down what you want to say and then review it to make sure it is clear and appropriate. Keep to the facts, focusing on the work not the person, and avoid emotional language (considering whether you would want to receive it in that way). Manage the situation, keeping in mind the following points:

- Honesty and sincerity are key concepts for such situations.
- Choose an appropriate context to deliver upsetting news.
- Ensure that enough time is available for discussion and consolation.
- Set expectations from the beginning by tone and words (be assertive, not confrontational).
- Find out what the person already recognises as inadequate in their work.
- Get to the point: do not delay but be clear and straightforward.
- If people become emotional, just stop and give them time and a place to compose themselves. Do not rush because you feel uncomfortable.
- Be sympathetic: let the other person know that you understand their distress.
- Respond to their reactions calmly and firmly.
- Provide details that support the decision. These should be provided in writing after any verbal delivery.
- Be prepared to answer questions about the problem(s).
- Note any positive outcomes that might mitigate or lessen the impact of the decision.

- Determine, and inform on, specific next steps, how they will be achieved and by whom.
- Help them to 'save face' when possible. Be mindful that they may be under pressure from elsewhere.
- Although the decision must be made with integrity, the way it is conveyed is important.
- Provide time and space for them to come to terms with the outcome.

The hardest part of collaborations and engaging with others is when people say they will do something but are not actually committed to delivering it or are unable to deliver on time or to the quality required. You may find people have different aims, agendas and/or time frames, so it is critical that you are aware of each other's positions, not just at the beginning, but also as the project unfolds. There may be a point in the project when the lack of deliverables or an inadequate response becomes critical; while planning contingency time into the project will mitigate such situations to an extent, there may come a point when you will know that you need to cut your losses and ask someone to step back from the project or reassign a task to save the project overall. This, of course, is only likely if you are leading a project or if you are responsible for others and it becomes apparent that keeping the individual in question will be detrimental to the outcome of the project or the effectiveness of the team. However, deadlines and consequences should all be agreed and determined in the beginning of a project, so that everyone is clear about what is required of them.

Being aware of what is happening or not working so well will serve you well in the future – you will recognise the signs in advance and anticipate the action that is required. You should be able to avoid critical situations like these if you are monitoring progress closely and are using that information to adapt and respond to the situation to improve continuously, making the necessary decisions in a timely way.

Different styles and persuading others

Not only will you need to listen to, and acknowledge, other people's viewpoints, but you will also need to be professionally confident and assertive. This means being clear about what you can give to a project as well as receive from it. Introverted personalities will have a different style from extroverts; however, no matter what your personality type, it is the outcome that you will all be focused on. Therefore, while extroverts may behave more gregariously and hold impromptu conversations, introverts may need to adopt more controlled strategies, such as holding regular meetings with clear agendas and implementing checklists to facilitate personal interaction, and so on. Irrespective of your style, you may need to be strategic and perhaps explicitly agree to meet some needs and not others or meet them at different stages. Above all, it will also mean that you will have the opportunity to hone your skills as a negotiator.

Negotiation skills will involve discussion and sharing, opening your mind to others and understanding what is important to them as much as to yourself. You also need to be persuasive. You may have to convince not only those involved in the work with you, but also those you report to and who may be responsible for your work (such as supervisors and PIs). Thus, you need to be alert to the fact that you may encounter some resistance to this activity (explored in Chapter 10), and so need to know how to put a business case for your involvement. Certainly, you should consider the advantages, disadvantages and benefits (or otherwise) of this activity, preferably evaluating them in a non-judgemental and professional way.

Monitoring and evaluation

Recording and monitoring benefits is becoming increasingly important for early-stage researchers as 'impact' chapters and statements are increasingly being required in submitted theses (this is discussed further in Chapter 6). More pertinently, statements concerning intended impact are vital in funding applications, so this would be an especially useful skill to acquire through your collaborative and/or engagement work when you have the opportunity to do so. In addition, funders will always want to know if you achieved the intended impact and will monitor your progress towards it via regular evaluative reports during the process. Consequently, learning to write such reports is also a useful skill to acquire. If you are not responsible for this, you could ask your supervisor or PI if you can help them, as a learning exercise, to produce one. Considering future impact, being able to make and/or write convincing and persuasive cases, and negotiating with others are all useful skills that can be obtained through collaborating and engaging.

Team working

If you are working with a team, you should cultivate an awareness of different kinds of team members and their styles. We all have different ways of working, so it is important to be as cognisant of your own preferences as well as those of your team members. From this, it is useful to reflect on how different ways of working might impact on other members and the performance of the team overall. What kind of team player are you? If you do not know, then you should seek some training or literature to help you establish a deeper understanding.

There are, fortunately, many different roles to play in a team, depending on the nature of the activity. Before you can utilise your strengths and those of the people around you, you will need to identify and establish an initial appreciation and understanding of the variety of roles (see Further Reading at the end of the chapter). Each role requires different approaches and skills, so there will be at least one role to match your current skills. Once you have gained some confidence from that, volunteer for one that takes you a little beyond your comfort zone so that you stretch yourself to learn more approaches and skills.

Of course, every project, including your current research project, will require an assessment of risk and ethical matters. You will also need an ongoing system for monitoring progress and performance, and for evaluating the quality of work outcomes. If you can achieve all the above, which it is entirely possible with collaborative and engagement work, then you will have an excellent skills base for managing the challenges we believe academia and any professional work area will face in the future. For instance, we anticipate academia will become more global and diverse, much like the business world already has. It will address larger research issues and topics, which will require researchers to adopt inclusive, interdisciplinary and mindful ways of working. Collaborating and engaging with others will provide you with ample opportunity to explore and extend your skills and abilities in these areas. It will also help to position you for meeting these challenges in the future. Try Activity 4.2 to begin to build an appreciation of your skill-set and attributes.

Activity 4.2

Spot the skills

Briefly scan the paragraphs in the above section on 'What key characteristics and skills are needed?' to identify and list all the skills that were mentioned. You can begin by seeking out the verbs, and then the qualities, behaviours and abilities in the above text.

How many have you spotted? We counted 70! (see Appendix B for details). Do not worry, though, if you do not have as many on your list.

Now tick all the ones you believe you are good at, and circle all those you are not so good at or have little or no experience in. This last group will give you an idea of where your professional development needs lie and which areas you can seek training or advice in next.

What are the main benefits for researchers?

Throughout this book we refer to some remarkable case studies and examples of the kinds of activity researchers have undertaken and the opportunities gained through collaborations and engaging with others. Many of the Voices of Experience illustrate the benefits, joys, surprises and challenges that such activities have afforded them, as illustrated in Voice of Experience 4.1.

Voice of Experience 4.1

Why I love collaborative projects!

I love working on international collaborative research projects because of the exposure to different lived experiences and landscapes that I would otherwise not have a good understanding of. There's a beauty in finding humans living in such different contexts and being in a position to exchange ideas and work together on projects that aim to improve livelihoods in impoverished communities.

Genevieve Agaba, PhD Agroforestry candidate, Bangor University

Researchers tend to find this activity fun and enjoyable, despite any difficulties they may encounter. Indeed, overcoming difficulties adds to a sense of pride and self-worth. If something is hard, like a doctorate, for instance, it produces a greater reward when accomplished than something relatively easy does.

The problem with a doctorate, though, is that it takes a long time to develop a sense of autonomy, and the outcomes can be abstract when they are eventually achieved. Collaborations and engagement activity can deliver more quickly a sense of ownership and personal value that derive from doing something that has tangible results and from encountering people outside normal day-to-day work. While the preceding sections in this chapter have framed this activity in the wider professional development context, we wish to underscore the point that this activity can be tremendously beneficial for you both personally and professionally.

In our experience, and that of experienced and specialist colleagues in these areas, collaborating and engaging with others are patently good for a researcher's self-esteem. Personally, it can be extremely supportive of your mental health and well-being, empowering you to feel good about yourself and your research. Working with the public, school children or organisations affords you the opportunity to exercise your own research voice and to develop independence, as well as confidence, in your work. Finding that people from outside your discipline are interested in your research project and in the researcher conducting it comes as a great revelation to many researchers. 'I never thought other people would be interested in my research' is a common comment we hear from researchers.

Thus, engaging in this activity can be very fulfilling for you (as Genevieve has discovered and illustrated in Voice of Experience 4.1). Getting involved with collaborative and/or engagement activity can enhance your professional (and personal) networks, broaden your experience of dealing with a diverse range of people and afford you the opportunity to experiment, play and grow (even if the lesson learned is not to respond in the same way in the future!).

Career advantages

Being involved in this activity is also advantageous for your career prospects. You will have an attractive item to add to your CV that will differentiate you from other researchers who lack experience beyond the academy. This can also be a source of specific interest to prospective employers, especially if they are interested in the contacts or outcomes of the collaborative work. In addition, many researchers who have been involved in placements in other sectors have valued the insight into different ways of working it has brought, and subsequently, in our experience, have often been offered good positions with the organisation (as indicated in Voice of Experience 3.3).

We discuss the benefits of placements further in Chapter 7, but it is useful to note here that placement experience may also impress prospective employers in other ways. For instance, non-academic employers will appreciate your insight into different working cultures as a result of a placement and of engaging with others. You may be better able to transition into another kind of working environment, particularly those with different priorities in terms of values and modes of working.

Collaborating and engaging others, then, not only develops the attributes that employers, including academic ones, are looking for, but also helps you to construct the proven track record that employers require. While of relevance to all researchers, this is especially important for postdoctoral researchers, who, by virtue of remaining longer in academia, will need to demonstrate a higher-level skill-set. These skills should include experience of leadership and the full range of management skills mentioned above. We understand the criticisms postdoctoral researchers sometimes make that, unless they have tenured positions, they are unable to be the PI on a project or may have limited access to funding in terms of eligibility. However, what is often not so well understood is that 'being the PI' is a leadership role. If you do not have any experience of leading 'something' related to research, you will remain at a disadvantage, not just in terms of funding, but also in terms of lacking the evidence that demonstrates your ability and track record through tangible results. Thus, collaborating, building relationships and partnerships and engaging with others can be especially beneficial to early-career researchers.

What can supervisors, PIs and institutions gain?

In this final section, we address doctoral supervisors, Principal Investigators (PIs) and those who have a wider stake or interest in researchers at the institutional level. Although the first point to note is that there has been very little formal research in this area, there is plenty of evidence – anecdotal and informal (all of which has saliency) – from researchers themselves, via blog posts, Twitter, and workshop and activity feedback, of how much they enjoy and have benefited from collaborative and engagement activity. '**Productive distractions**' (Harris, 2018: 168), such as collaborative working and engaging with others, is clearly good for researchers' mental health and well-being. These are areas of national and international concern (see Further Reading at the end of the chapter), so that this kind of activity must be taken more seriously by doctoral supervisors, PIs and, more widely, by institutions.

We would advise, then, that PIs, supervisors and institutions build opportunities for collaborating and/or engagement work into the thesis or postdoctoral research time to enhance their research efforts, rather than viewing it as distracting researchers from the task of conducting research. This activity should become an integral element of the research process, not least for the personal and professional benefits it brings, which can manifest in three ways: for the researcher (as discussed in the previous sections in this chapter), for the supervisor and/or PI, and for the institution, as we indicate next.

Collaborative working and engaging with others are excellent vehicles for facilitating the kind of independence that all researchers aim for and that their supervisors/PIs aspire for them too. There is much that can be leveraged in terms of learning and experience for researchers in this respect. These kinds of activity often increase self-confidence and enthusiasm for the research, while supervisors and PIs can play a central role by encouraging participation and by providing reassurance, guidance and support throughout. Researchers may need help to understand that they are ambassadors for their institution or project, and that there will be limitations to authority in this regard. Furthermore, supervisors and PIs may need to ensure that researchers understand that they cannot over-promise resources or compromise intellectual property or the institution in any-way, all of which are perfect topics for research training too.

In short, this form of activity is good for overall professional development. It enables and develops a wider and more mature skill-set than can often be achieved by focusing on the research alone. In Chapter 9 we discuss some practical ways in which collaborative and wider engagement can be facilitated.

For any supervisor, PI or institution concerned with employability (particularly if you are worried that the researcher may not be suited for an academic career and do not know what to do about that), then providing or encouraging the researcher to undertake an external experience, such as a placement, could prove highly benefi-cial. Despite the lack of research and data in this area, we have learnt from external engagements that when timed appropriately in the researcher life-cycle, they can, in the words of one public engagement lead at a university, 'accelerate completion rates' for doctoral researchers and 'propel them towards finishing' (anonymised). Frequently, researchers appear to recognise the additional value in their research which would not have occurred to them while sitting at a computer screen or at a lab bench, immersed in its detail rather than its bigger picture.

Encouraging researchers to undertake collaborative and engagement work can also be of benefit to doctoral supervisors and PIs. At one level, it will extend your connections and perhaps also your knowledge, which we know supervisors espe-cially value about working with their doctoral researchers. It can also prepare the ground for policy-influencing activity and collaborating with a host of external groups to develop further research that you may be interested in exploring your-self. Doctoral and postdoctoral researchers can undertake background research on your behalf or make initial enquiries and connections if you do not have time to do this yourself.

Initiating such discussions and managing relationships and administration is time-consuming even if your institution has an office that can assist with estab-lishing connections with policy makers, industries or other external organisations, such as a Research and Innovation office or an **Enterprise office**. Nevertheless, this does provide a development opportunity to a researcher unfamiliar with such processes. It is vitally important that postdoctoral researchers enhance their pro-fessional abilities and do so at a higher level than a doctoral researcher may need. Therefore, we would especially encourage PIs to look for ways in which to work with postdoctoral researchers, similar perhaps to the ICURe model we illustrated in Chapter 3. To capitalise on these opportunities for your researchers, consider Reflection Point 4.1.

Reflection Point 4.1

What opportunities can supervisors and PIs create?

Consider the research project(s) you are working on currently. Are there areas where you would like to explore possibilities with policy makers, businesses, educators, charities and communities, but that you do not have time for? Could you create an opportunity for your doctoral or postdoctoral researcher here that can be mutually beneficial? If so, what tasks would you like them to undertake on your behalf? What information could they prepare for you?

You may find yourself providing support, guidance and advice in important areas, such as ethical and professional conduct, Intellectual Property and management of difficult situations, rather than managing or controlling or leading on every initiative. Indeed, this might provide the occasion for a collaborative, rather than a cooperative, relationship. The lesson here for everyone is that more is gained by sharing and including, and by not rigidly adhering to established notions of hierarchical relationships.

PIs and supervisors, then, may need to adopt a humbler approach in their relationships with the researchers they work with when undertaking these activities. This of course implies an inclusive style of leadership and a flatter approach to team or people management. Be prepared to recognise that engaging and collaborating disrupts the established order and hierarchy, which we urge everyone to embrace rather than feel threatened by. In the end, the benefits and enjoyment this kind of research work brings can be very inspiring, and frequently in unexpected ways. Reflection Point 4.2 asks you to consider some awkward questions in this area.

Reflection Point 4.2

What is the real anxiety?

A common objection to extra-curricular activity from academic staff is, as mentioned earlier, that it is a 'distraction' from the research. Let us consider this objection for a moment:

- What assumptions are being made about the ability of researchers to manage their commitments?
- What is the real fear or underlying anxiety here?
- If this is your current view, or one you have held in the past, how true is/was it that the research would not be completed? What evidence do/did you have?

There is a challenging question here about how well everyone (supervisor, PI and researchers included) know, understand and appreciate each other's perspectives. Is there an opportunity for everyone to explore these further? What would need to change to make this a 'win-win' situation for you and the researcher?

Contemplate for a moment Voice of Experience 4.2, that of a senior, experienced researcher who took up the challenge effectively for her and her researchers' benefit.

Voice of Experience 4.2

Never too old to learn

Even before it became an issue for supervisors of doctoral researchers, indeed, throughout my research career, I have been pretty obsessed about completing on time, whether it be my own research projects or those I was supervising. I am one of those with regular meetings and check points set up in my online diary to ensure that progress goes to plan.

Thus, it came as a challenge to me when a researcher came to me with a suggestion that he engage local pharmacists to explore why patients seem not to take their medication as recommended. He was thrilled to have been recommended by his own pharmacist, who knew he was studying 'social biosciences' and so 'knew how to do research'. He was so enthusiastic, despite my concerns about the impact of this activity on the time-scale for his doctorate, that I couldn't refuse. To be honest, he put so much effort into designing the questionnaire for these pharmacists that he became the person of choice to send other new researchers to when they considered using survey techniques.

In fact, his links were so successful that later we were both invited to contribute to the Pharmaceutical Society's work on Medicine Use Review. It was great to see him transform from being a university student into a professional researcher working for the community. That transformation also had an impact on his doctorate because he became more self-assured and organised as he juggled his academic and community role and, in fact, submitted his thesis several months ahead of time.

Emeritus Professor

Aside from perhaps improving completion rates, collaborations and engagement can enhance and extend the activity and reputation of institutions, although the extent to which institutions are conscious of this remains unclear. There is a tendency, naturally, for institutions to take a top-level approach to such activity, for instance, by being more interested in large and prestigious partnerships and promoting their high-level international collaborations on their websites. Yet, as was mentioned in Chapter 1, if impactful work originates with doctoral and post-doctoral researchers, there might be opportunities here that institutions have not fully considered, as identified in Voice of Experience 4.2.

The connections and networks that enthusiastic researchers create, and which extend way beyond academia, are of consequence to institutions and can be of interest to Senior Management Teams (SMTs). Many of these 'stories' from researchers prepare the ground for impact case studies, support REF-type submissions and other institutional narratives, and indicate the rich and vibrant research community that institutions have generated and which contribute to the wider society. Certainly, we would say that the connections international researchers and alumni bring can open the way to global public engagement activity, and we are aware of one institution that has worked with alumni to set up events with schools in their home countries. Leaving to one side the benefits this may have for student recruitment, we envisage significant potential benefit in this international development. Who knows what incredible opportunities might be generated on the back of the collaborations and engagement work researchers undertake?

Not only is collaborating and engaging good for researchers and for their institutions, but we firmly believe that a 'good' university will encourage and actively provide structural support for this activity. Structural support, we suggest, includes:

- Openly celebrating the collaborations and engagements researchers are involved in
- Acknowledging the value of this activity as a critical part of university business
- Providing relevant training and development opportunities for researchers and their supervisors and PIs
- Making space for this in the research programme or contract (for example, the 10 days training per annum for researchers that UK institutions set aside)
- Recognise the added value to the institution by assessing the business benefits; even a simple enquiry into this would be a step towards endorsing this form of activity.

Changes in attitude among staff and researchers in this area, as well as institutional recognition and structural support, all serve to confirm that the researcher role and higher education landscape are shifting, as we indicated at the beginning of this book. One area that clearly signifies this change, and which has generated extensive growth in activity while being enormously popular among researchers, is public engagement, which we examine in more detail in our next two chapters.

Further reading

Belbin, M.R. (2010) *Team Roles at Work* (2nd edition). London and New York: Routledge.

Cain, S. (2013) *Quiet: The Power of Introverts in a World that Can't Stop Talking.* London: Penguin Books.

Harris, Z., in Denicolo, D., Reeves, J. and Duke, D. (2018) *Success in Research: Fulfilling the Potential of Your Doctoral Experience.* London: SAGE.

Richards, M., Elliott, A., Woloshyn, V. and Mitchell, C. (2001) *Collaboration Uncovered: The Forgotten, the Assumed, and the Unexamined in Collaborative Education.* Westport, CT: Bergin & Garvey.

Vitae, in partnership with the Institute for Employment Studies (IES) and the University of Ghent (2018) *Exploring Wellbeing and Mental Health and Associated Support Services for Postgraduate Researchers.* Located at: https://re.ukri.org/documents/2018/mental-health-report/ (retrieved 31/03/2019).

Walsh, L. and Kahn, P. (eds) (2010) *Collaborative Working in Higher Education: The Social Academy.* New York and London: Routledge.

5

How can doctoral and postdoctoral researchers engage with the public?

In this chapter you are invited to consider:

- The context of public engagement
- The variety of public engagement activity
- Some issues you need to be aware of when engaging with the public
- Some of the distinct benefits public engagement offers
- Key points when designing and evaluating engagement activity
- Some exciting and emergent trends

As highlighted in Chapters 2 and 3, there are many structured opportunities for doctoral and postdoctoral researchers to engage with the public, either directly relating to their research or more generally. This chapter will specifically focus on how to engage the public with research, looking at potential audiences and the benefits of engaging in this way.

The public engagement context

An area that has seen tremendous growth in its range and variety of activity over the past decade or so has been in community or public engagement. For doctoral and postdoctoral researchers, this form of engagement is increasingly attractive not simply due to this variety of activity, but also due to the apparent freedom associated with public engagement. We know of researchers, from every discipline and at all career stages, who have engaged the public with posters in museums and public houses, performed stand-up comedy routines, entertained families and school-children with interactive talks and hands-on experiments, and who have worked with charities, organisations and special interest groups to produce better research outcomes. The range of activity is truly inspiring. In contrast to the more traditional engagement activities within academia that are accompanied by formal legal contracts and permissions, public engagement does not apparently require such formalised considerations.

We say apparently because, as you will see below, there will always be ethical considerations and if you are working with children or vulnerable adults, criminal background checks – and perhaps even health and safety considerations too – all of which are often as weighty as those required with collaborative work. For instance, the simple idea of inviting local school children to visit your department or institution to hear a tea-time lecture (which is a great idea and one that is often done by postdoctoral researchers) will require you to consider, at the very least, any risks to the children while they are on campus. In addition, there will be transportation, health and safety and comfort matters to attend to.

In the UK, there has been a veritable explosion of public engagement activity both by academic staff and researchers. Much of this activity has been driven by public demand for greater transparency of research. Areas where this demand is evident include national policy initiatives, especially those that require the impact of research to be shared more widely, and projects supported through public funding, leading to public interest in the value to society of such projects. As a consequence of this increased public interest in research, what ostensibly began life as 'communicating science' to a wider audience, especially school children, has expanded to encompass all areas of academia and society. It would be unusual to find no form of public engagement activity in an institution or even a single department these days.

While academic staff may have a whole range of reasons for engaging with the public, researchers can simply enjoy it for what it is. Doctoral and postdoctoral researchers alike can engage, explore and experiment with, entertain and explain to the public more freely, largely immune from the direct demands of funders to demonstrate value for money, or from the need to evidence the impact of their research by participating in national assessment processes such as the Research Excellence Framework (REF). Any visit to a science festival or university open day for families will confirm that the value of such engagement often is nothing other than the simple joy it can bring. As illustrated in Voice of Experience 10.2 in Chapter 10, this form of engagement enhances a sense of self-worth and well-being. While institutions, supervisors and PIs may not yet fully recognise the value and benefit that public engagement brings to doctoral and postdoctoral researchers, there is no reason for you not to realise this.

Getting started with public engagement activities

UK Universities and research organisations (as signatories to the Manifesto for Public Engagement, discussed further in Chapter 6) have typically adopted the definition of public engagement coined by the National Coordinating Centre for Public Engagement (NCCPE): 'Engagement is by definition a two-way process, involving interaction and listening, with the goal of generating mutual benefit.'

In their public engagement and other collaborative endeavours, universities typically work with a wide range of organisations and groups within the public sector and civil society. Those people or groups who might have an interest in your research – stakeholders if you prefer – are wide-ranging, and many may already have connections to your institutions, a department or individual member of academic staff. We invite you, in Activity 5.1, to think about who the potential stakeholders for your research project are.

Activity 5.1

Identifying stakeholders or possible 'publics'

Consider the list below and tick the boxes for each group you think might have an interest in your research, who you could talk to or who you could engage with your research.

Possible public groups or stakeholders	Tick all those you could engage with
Schools and colleges	
Businesses	
Health groups and charitable societies	
Medical groups (doctors, hospitals)	
Political groups or organisations	
Charities	
Voluntary groups	
Cultural groups – creative industries	
Leisure, health and fitness groups	
Community associations and groups	
Media	
Any others?	

It is helpful to keep in mind these different potential stakeholders so that you can start to explore the opportunities and connections that may already exist within your institution; these may inform how you can get started with public engagement yourself. Many UK universities have a presence at high-profile national festivals. For example, the Economic and Social Research Council (ESRC) have facilities at the Cheltenham Festival (horse-racing venue), the Festival of Social Science and Glastonbury (music) Festival, while the Arts and Humanities Research Council (AHRC) hosts the Being Human Festival in partnership with the University of London. Other universities are actively involved in regional or local community/outreach events and may even run their own large-scale events.

Outside the UK, there will be similar events and institutional connections. Quite often these are connected to environmental and/or health issues, such as water-testing days for local communities or hand-washing campaigns. A wonderful example is the Science-Express in India (see www.sciencexpress.in/). This 16-coach train is a mobile science exhibition supported by the Department of Science and Technology. It raises awareness of issues such as climate change and aims to introduce young people to a range of science and technology subjects.

Increasingly, public engagement teams within universities are coordinating and helping to deliver a range of opportunities for researchers to engage with people outside the institution, often in partnership with other organisations (museums, community groups, schools and colleges, for example). These initiatives will be shaped by the character, size and location of the institution, and its mission statement and values.

Doctoral or early-career researchers can volunteer to be part of the delivery team without necessarily having been involved in the planning and design of the activity or exhibit. This, small initial step, can be an excellent way to test out your aptitude, hone your communications skills and see how other researchers deal with tasks. By starting as a volunteer on someone else's team, you can gain ideas and insights which can be helpful in your own subsequent engagement practice. Depending on the openings available, you may also get an opportunity to design and test a small contribution of your own as part of a larger/wider team. Being part of an established team/activity can also help to connect you with other organisations and groups outside the university, enabling you to develop some networks of your own over time. However, before you get started, even as a volunteer on an established engagement activity, there are some things you must be alert to when working with the public.

What do you need to know about working with the public?

At the heart of public engagement is an admirable concept: sharing the benefit of ideas with others. However, this is not a neutral stance; it can be a 'political' one and it is certainly a philosophical one. It is important to recognise that your view and definition of a good idea or initiative is simply that – your view. It may not be shared by others, whether they are in academia or beyond in the wider society. Just as your ideas may not be accepted by fellow researchers – indeed, that is what schools of thought and debate about epistemologies are for – the public may also not be interested or may reject your overtures entirely. This concept may be more familiar to researchers in HASS disciplines who are used to critique, but all researchers need to be aware of their motivations and personal values that inform any engagement with the public.

The public are not an empty vessel waiting for you to correct their 'mistaken' ideas. Certainly, in the current and sad climate of 'suspicion of experts', the wise researcher will both tread and listen carefully. The importance of being careful in these respects reinforces the need to be compassionate and curious about others, as we suggested in the Collaborative Code in Chapter 1, and to be reflective about our own motivations and values. Reflection Point 5.1 may help you to consider what your deeper values and motivations for public engagement are.

Reflection Point 5.1

Exploring your motivations and values

Reflect on the following questions:

- Why do you want to engage with the public?
- Why is this important to you?
- What do you want to achieve?
- How would you feel if the public disagrees with, or rejects, your initiative?

Some of the insights from Chapter 2 on taking small steps and seeking out training and support from within your institution are salient here too. There may be training opportunities and resources available nationally, via funders (such as the Research Councils UK) or other sector organisations. Also, enquire about what is available within your institution or whether your university or department can be persuaded to acquire training provision. Participating in training can go in tandem with getting hands-on experience; often there is training connected with a particular engagement activity, or a training course will culminate in an opportunity to put skills into practice. Voice of Experience 5.1 illustrates how training can then lead researchers to meet school children in a safe environment.

Voice of Experience 5.1

The benefits of engaging with school children

I have been the Programme Manager for LifeLab for 10 years. LifeLab is an innovative educational intervention, actively engaging teenagers and teachers with science to explain how lifestyle choices at an early age drastically affect future health. Another aim is to offer opportunities to become enthusiastic about science, considering further study and careers. The education community is proactive in promoting science as a career, and yet curriculum constraints hamper efforts to bring 'science to life' for teenagers, particularly girls and those in more disadvantaged areas, who don't see science as relevant for their lives. When asked to describe science/scientists, teenagers use words implying an exclusive club which is inaccessible to them.

So, I developed a scheme which is now embedded in our activities called 'Meet the Scientist'. Doctoral and postdoctoral researchers provide opportunities for school students to sit and chat in small, informal groups with different researchers. The 'Meet the Scientist' initiative attempts to bridge the gap between students carrying out their secondary education in the UK and researchers at higher education institutions, providing secondary-level school students with opportunities not just to meet and talk to scientists, but also to explore or challenge their views of scientists.

The researchers receive a day's training and plan their interactions carefully with the help of teachers, as working with teenagers is often a new experience for them. Follow-up with the students shows that this short interaction with researchers can have a powerful impact, especially for female students, as this comment shows: 'School promotes female scientists, but only after actually meeting young women scientists did I realise it could be a possibility for me.'

We are always so overwhelmed by the support of our scientists and their willingness to give up their time to inspire and interact with the next generation. However, what is apparent is the impact on the researchers themselves, with the questions and interactions with the school students encouraging reflection from the researchers on their own research:

'It [participating in a 'Meet the Scientist' session] helped me think about how to communicate my work; their [the school students] feedback was more mature than I had expected...'

'It made me think in a different way about my research...'

'It kept me going when I had challenging times in my PhD; it reminded me why I loved doing my science.'

Dr Kathryn Woods-Townsend, LifeLab Programme Manager,
University of Southampton Education School

As indicated in Voice of Experience 5.1, the benefits of public engagement are multi-layered and experienced by both the public and the researchers. The benefits that derive from public engagement for researchers participating in this form of activity require further investigation and appreciation, especially from an institutional perspective.

What are the benefits to researchers?

Engaging with the public can be exhilarating: not only will you find people from all walks of life interested in research, but the variety of viewpoints you will encounter may raise questions about your work or issues about which you may not have been aware of previously. Consequently, it can help you gain new perspectives on your research. Certainly, addressing the unexpected questions that the public, especially school children, can raise will challenge the way you think and respond. This is good practical experience for any doctoral researcher facing a viva voce.

In Chapter 4 we considered the personal and professional benefits to researchers of collaborating and engaging more generally. In this chapter, we wish to highlight that focusing on public engagement will further enhance these benefits. At a personal level, engaging with the public can be immensely rewarding and satisfying as well as self-affirming. Certainly, we have seen how engaging with the public can boost researchers' confidence and morale. Moreover, it can be both developmental and fun. Information Box 5.1 contains two contrasting examples of public engagement, which are equally enjoyable and rewarding for the researcher.

Information Box 5.1

Bright and Brilliant researchers

There are two national schemes in the UK that provide training and support in two different areas:

The Bright Club (www.brightclub.org/). Describes itself as 'The Thinking Person's Variety Night'. The organisation provides researchers with the opportunity to perform stand-up comedy acts based on their research. Even the most unlikely of subjects, from batteries to black holes to wasps, can entertain the public with a bit of help and support!

The Brilliant Club (https://thebrilliantclub.org/). Helps doctoral researchers deliver courses and educational materials in schools. They provide teacher-training and arrange for researchers to work with teaching staff in less advantaged schools and areas. Their aim is to inspire pupils from under-represented backgrounds to progress to university.

Both the schemes mentioned in Information Box 5.1 provide training and established (as well as safe) environments for researchers to engage with the public, albeit in very different ways. Both enable researchers to refine their skill-sets further.

Reflection Point 5.2

Is all skills enhancement the same?

Reflecting on the public engagement opportunities that the Brilliant Club and the Bright Club offer to researchers, reflect on the following questions:

- What personal and professional skills and other attributes do you think teaching and stand-up comedy enhance?
- Would the enhancement be the same, or would these differing forms of engagement strengthen different kinds of skill?
- How might each of these activities, or something similar, advance your skills?

A useful starting point for assessing your own public engagement skill-set is the *Attributes Framework for Public Engagement* developed by Johnson, Williams and Manners (2010). This framework focuses on the three key areas of communication, empathy and reflection, and then details the attributes. Keep in mind that attributes, as we discussed in Chapter 4, are set in the context of specific behaviours that are learned as part of external experiences; in other words, they can be practised, developed and refined. It is worth looking at the framework closely, as it may well have informed any training or support that is currently available at your institution, especially if you are in the UK. For researchers elsewhere, you might want to introduce the framework within your institution. Activity 5.2 invites you to compare the skills you identified in Chapter 4 with those in the framework.

Activity 5.2

Skills revisited

In Activity 4.2 you were asked to 'spot the skills' that you could develop or enhance by undertaking collaborative and engagement work. Look at the list again, as well as the items you ticked as being good at, and compare those with the skills in the *Attributes Framework for Public Engagement*, which you can find online (see Further Reading at the end of this chapter).

One reason for becoming involved in public engagement is the informal learning that it affords, which may even lead to employment opportunities, as indicated in Voice of Experience 5.2.

Voice of Experience 5.2

Why I love public engagement!

I discovered public engagement during my PhD, and I rapidly got hooked. I started by giving talks and then delivering stand-up comedy as part of the Bright Club. This was something I never imagined I would do. Public engagement really helped to re-enthuse me about my subject as well. Doing a PhD is hard work, and you need something fun to keep you going. I found myself working with the loveliest of people.

The best bit was when I was offered a job working between the university and local schools, which was as a direct result of my public engagement experience. I had no idea such jobs even existed. My advice to all researchers is to do public engagement activities at some point during your research. Who knows what it might lead to?

Dr Jessica Spurrell, School-University Partnership Officer, University of Southampton

Another important aspect of public engagement is that not only does it raise the profile of your research, but it also enhances the reputation of your institution in so far as the relationships you create and levels of trust you establish will reflect positively on your institution. Furthermore, this activity is currently creating new roles and, in some universities, expanded teams. This employment trend will be aligned to an institution's strategic goals, and if, as is the case in one or two institutions (the University of Manchester and Herriot Watt University, for example), community engagement and/or social responsibility are perceived as being of strategic importance, then these are the kinds of institutions to look out for if you wish to continue working in this area. This highlights another benefit to researchers: it is increasing the range of possible researcher careers.

If we have succeeded in capturing your interest in these activities, then you should read on to discover more about how to progress beyond thinking it is an interesting idea.

Designing public engagement practice: purpose, people and process

Once you have reached a point where you want to start developing your own public engagement practice, there are some key elements to consider. At the outset, decide exactly what you wish to achieve through engaging with others. The focus now should be on your purpose rather than your motives. It is easy to get carried away with an exciting idea or activity, or to look at what others are doing and feel under pressure to do something similar, rather than carving your own niche.

It can be tempting to think in terms of the 'general public' when starting to plan, but this broad-brush approach to selecting an audience is unlikely to enable an effective and meaningful interaction which achieves your desired objectives. Being clear on your engagement purpose will help you to identify who to engage with; that is, it will define who your 'public' should be. Once you are clear on your purpose and your target audience, you can work out the best method/time/place ('process') to engage them. See Information Box 5.2 for examples of how a different purpose will determine the people and the process to engage with.

Information Box 5.2

Purpose, people and process

The following examples show how a different purpose will dictate the people and the process involved in engaging:

'I need to encourage participation in my study. This is more likely if potential participants have more information, so I will create a series of podcasts for my website to provide this in an easily accessible way.'

'I need to encourage more participation in our Public Astronomy Evenings later this year, and I think that running a family-friendly workshop for the upcoming Festival of Wonder will help to raise interest and pull in a larger audience.'

'To enhance my research in xxx and identify new/potential directions, I want to meet and talk to people who have a lived experience of xxx so that I can learn from them and see what their ideas are.'

While you may have an idea of what you would like to do, you will still need to explore whether this is appropriate for your prospective audience. This will mean finding out about them in advance and then finding ways to meet them. When considering how you might best engage a specific audience or group, it is useful to ask the following questions:

- Where do they go or spend time?
- What do they read, watch and/or do?

- Who do they interact or connect with?
- What does your prospective audience have in common with you?
- What would they be most apprehensive and excited about?

In addition, when planning your engagement process, there are many formats you can consider in relation to your objectives and your target audience. NCCPE's Typology of Public Engagement Processes (see below) provides a useful overview and suggests the following possible formats:

- Lecture/presentation, broadcast, event
- Writing, encounter, website
- Performance, exhibition, exhibit
- Workshop, network, social media
- Collaboration, consultation, formal learning
- Citizen research, collaborative research, collaborative enquiry

You can find out more about these on the NCCPE's website (their 'process' page: www.publicengagement.ac.uk/do-engagement/quality-engagement/process), which includes useful links to case studies showing how different processes can support different purposes and audiences.

In designing an event – even a talk to a local community group – you should establish what you would like to do, the purpose of it, why it should be you doing it, and the way you could participate while engaging people. You will probably be doing this with other people, ideally with the support and encouragement of your supervisor and PI, and ideally will have received some training or advice too. Activity 5.3 invites you to imagine engaging with a range of publics.

Activity 5.3

What would be an engaging experience for you?

In Information Box 5.1 we showed you two very different ways to engage an audience – teaching and comedy. The range of possibilities for engaging people seems to be limited only by imagination. However, some of the ways might include an exhibition, interactive models, an interactive experience and storytelling.

Consider in what creative ways you can engage the following:

- A class of 14-year-old pupils
- A local branch of the Alzheimer's Society
- Parents and children

- Your local book club
- A group of retired citizens

Now, list all the things that you might need to consider, or obtain advice or approval for, if you were to engage each audience in that way.

When you have ideas, your audience, the format of the event and colleagues to help or support you, you will still need to consider if there are any health and safety, Intellectual Property, ethical or legal issues to be aware of. This is the case for all forms of external engagement, as highlighted in Chapter 3. Again, you should consider if there are any gender or environmental impacts too. None of this need be complex or difficult; it is simply a matter of being mindful of what you are doing and with whom, and ultimately it is about creating an enjoyable and fun time for all involved.

Success and impact

Once you are happy with your objective(s), audience and process, you need to consider how you will measure success against your desired outcome(s): how will you know that your engagement activity has been successful? How will you evidence this? Although it is tempting to start your activity/project right away, assuming that evaluation is something you do afterwards, it is essential to build evaluation and measurement into your planning from the beginning. You need to take the same approach as you would when planning a class or teaching materials. In short, start with the desired result and work backwards.

Public engagement and research impact

The evaluation of public engagement is as creative a process as designing the event itself. Obviously, you could ask people how they felt about the event, what they learned, and so on, but if you are part of a large event, such as a festival, that might be challenging both for the participants to differentiate your part in the whole event and for you to track them down. However, you will want to obtain some evidence of the impact (subsequent after effect) and benefit of your collective effort.

The UK Research Excellence Framework (REF) defines impact as: 'an effect on, change or benefit to the economy, society, culture, public policy or services, health, the environment or quality of life, beyond academia' (Research England, https://re.ukri.org/research/ref-impact/). These are significant items to capture, particularly as the REF looks for both *reach* and *significance;* that is the extent, depth, range and importance of the impact achieved. As a doctoral and post-doctoral researcher, evaluating, assessing and capturing evidence of any impact, presents another informal opportunity to acquire a new and highly useful skill. You can learn by asking to be involved in the evaluation process and discussions about impact conducted by those leading public engagement events or by enquiring about other people's experience. Many of the REF 2014 impact case studies contained some element of public engagement and are available online (https://impact.ref.ac.uk/casestudies/). Further, Jon Copley (2018) shares his experience in a paper of a successful impact case study based on a programme of informative/inspiring-type public engagement that you may find useful too (see Further Reading at the end of this chapter).

The detail of any evaluation will depend on the purpose, audience and type of engagement being undertaken. It can be woven into activities, conducted at intervals, can be **formative** and/or **summative**, light-touch or in-depth. The evaluation methods selected need to suit the engagement itself, paying heed to the time frame, the resources available and who may want or need to see the evidence of your success, such as partners, stakeholders, funders, your supervisor or PI. The evaluation data/information collected can encompass both the quantitative (such as numbers of participants, attendees, footfall, website hits and analytics) and the qualitative (comments, opinions, responses, conversations, informal exchanges, stories of change), and will vary according to the purpose of the engagement and the nature of the audience.

Designing an evaluation provides another stage in the collaborative and engagement processes from which you can gain. The opportunity for you to observe, gather information and learn from others while being involved in a fun activity, are all part of the informal learning process that enable doctoral and postdoctoral researchers to position themselves for future roles.

Following up to maintain engagement

We will consider following up in more detail in Chapter 11. Here we raise a few points that will be useful for you to consider. At a minimum it is polite to thank everyone for their involvement or participation – personal thanks are always appreciated. However, this may not be possible following a large event. So other means, for instance a notice at the exit or email afterwards, may be preferable.

If you wish to strengthen or continue any collaboration or encounter you have had with people, following up appropriately will be vital. This will be especially important for those (mostly supervisors and PIs) interested in capturing evidence of the impact of the engagement, but will also be useful for doctoral and postdoctoral researchers to be aware of because public engagement activities can often require a more proactive follow-up, unlike academic collaboration and engagement in which the impact can be seen in proposals written, papers submitted or events organised.

Diligent follow-up also allows you to build your brand and increase your 'collaboration readiness' (see Appendix A) by strengthening your network and making your name recognisable for future activities. Each contact point you have with the public is an opportunity to build connectivity and solidify trust (which we discuss further in Chapter 8), while all of these may contain the seeds of further activity. Information Box 5.3 provides some ideas to help you create a consistent 'personal brand'. This will make it easier for the public, even in a very simple way, to identify you and find out more about your public engagement activity. Basically, as in academia, you need to promote yourself in a consistent and coherent way.

Information Box 5.3

Building a consistent brand

One of the key challenges when working with any group of people, of any age, is ensuring that your messages and communication with them is relevant and consistent. Considering how you have promoted yourself (or a project) to the outside world, ask yourself if your message or 'brand' is consistent:

- **Is your content error-free?** Spend some time checking for, and fixing, errors in any existing webpages, accounts and posts.
- **Do you use a style guide for your emails or newsletters?** Consistent formatting will not only save you time, but also strengthen your brand recognition by balancing quality and scale. You can ask your institution's public engagement office, or even your department administrator, for ideas on style guides you could try.
- **Do you have a systemised sign-up, registration or forms submission process?** For example, do you use Eventbrite consistently for all your event sign-ups? If you have never used these before, check with others who have and get a better sense of what might work best for you. You may have preference to use Google Forms if everything else you use is in Google, for example.
- **Do you use a variety of methods for engagement follow-up?** You can consider this as multi-channel marketing of your brand. The more varied your audience, the more varied you may need to consider making your follow-up. Not only will this

(Continued)

help you reach your wider audience, but it will afford opportunities to reinforce your brand. Be ready to use email, mobile, social media and even traditional mail, allowing your audience to choose which methods they prefer.

- **Do you know what gets attention?** Have you already used analytics to check your website activity or link hits? Are there commonalities between when (is there an optimal time of day to send your updates) or what (are certain topics getting all the likes?) people click on? You can start testing this with your next email update as an example. Email half of your list in the morning and the other half in the afternoon. You can then track which got read or which websites were accessed the most and use this information to inform when best to send emails to your entire group.
- **Do you offer transparency in your interactions?** For example, is your blog up to date and does it give readers a true representation of your work?
- **Have you spoken to the public or your intended audience?** Have you taken feedback from them? Do you know what they are interested in or want from you?

Engagement activities offer a wealth of potential for collaboration and, perhaps, un-anticipated opportunities such as new connections or career openings. You may be surprised to learn that there are also many avenues to find funding and support for these activities. Your own institution may have internal resources or awards for community development, engaging with industry, outreach activities, and so on. Increasingly, national organisations and research funders are supporting this activity financially, which is a trend we all welcome, leading us to consider what other future trends are emerging.

Future trends?

Most of the discussion above has been determined by the notion that you will be presenting something to an audience. That audience may have helped to shape the event or activity, but usually it is the research or the researcher who provides the impetus for the engagement. This comes back to the discussion we had in Chapter 1 when we drew a distinction between collaboration and engagement and suggested that engagement need not involve mutual design. Indeed, much activity involves sharing information or seeking information that improves the research, such as through a consultation or opinion polls. There is a well-known diagram by the Wellcome Trust called the 'Public Engagement Onion' that, in a series of layers like an onion, depicts a range of activity that moves from holding a genuine dialogue with people to giving out information to them. Giving information to, or inspiring, people can be done by providing a lecture or organising a festival, while a dialogue will involve the public in decision making about research.

One of the most interesting trends is in the area of dialogue and in actively engaging the public not just in the research, but also in the initial setting of research questions and in the co-design of research. The issue of co-design and co-production of research with the public sees engagement and collaboration merge together. This can be an exciting space in which researchers can work.

Another exciting trend is in international public engagement. While the model of café scientific (www.cafescientifique.org/) is already a global one, researchers are taking their public engagement further. International researchers, with knowledge and connections in their home countries, are either undertaking public engagement work from their host institution (as an international form of outreach) or supporting it as alumni when they return home. This is set to provide even more opportunity for researchers.

Research for All is a relatively new open-access, peer-reviewed journal focusing on research that involves universities and communities, services and/or industries working together. It has wide-ranging articles, from diverse authors and vantage-points, highlighting the potential for robust academic study within public engagement. The development of research in this area is warmly welcomed. Whatever the future holds, it looks set to be a rich one for researchers in terms of public engagement.

In the next chapter we consider the implications of the UK experience further to discern what can be learned and be of benefit elsewhere.

Further reading

Barnett, C. and Mahony, N. (September 2011) *Segmenting Publics*. Retrieved from: www.publicengagement.ac.uk/sites/default/files/publication/segmenting_publics_2_nov_2011.pdf

Copley, J. (2018) Providing evidence of impact from public engagement with research: a case study from the UK's Research Excellence Framework (REF). *Research for All*, 2(2), July.

Hart, A., Northmore, S. and Gerhardt, C. (2009) *Briefing Paper: Auditing, Benchmarking and Evaluating Public Engagement*. Retrieved from: www.publicengagement. ac.uk/sites/default/files/publication/evaluatingpublicengagement_1.pdf

Johnson, B., Williams, B. and Manners, P. (2010) *DRAFT Attributes Framework for Public Engagement for University Staff and Students*. Retrieved from: www. publicengagement.ac.uk/sites/default/files/publication/an_attributes_framework_for_public_engagement_december_2010_0_0.pdf

Rask, M. et al. (2016) *Innovative Public Engagement: A Conceptual Model of Public Engagement in Dynamic and Responsible Governance of Research and Innovation*.

Report on the ThePE2020 project (2014–2017). Retrieved from: https://pe2020.eu/wp-content/uploads/2016/05/Innovative-Public-Engagement-FINAL-1.pdf

Research England (n.d.) *REF Impact* website. https://re.ukri.org/research/ref-impact/ (accessed 17 August 2019)

Research Excellence Framework: REF 2014. *Impact case studies* website (contains over 6,000 case studies in a searchable database). https://impact.ref.ac.uk/casestudies/ (accessed 17 August 2019)

6

What can we learn from public engagement?

Guest author: Jo James

In this chapter we invite you to explore:

- The place of public engagement in the wider context
- The strategic and cultural drivers which have shaped both the concept and practice of public engagement within the UK academy through recent decades
- How these developments are playing out within doctoral research
- Their potential implications for the doctorate

The concept of 'public engagement' (sharing the conception, activity and benefits of research with the public) is by no means exclusive to the UK, as we indicated in the previous chapter, although in other countries the term 'community engagement' is more commonly found. A global study (see Hall et al., 2015) of over 50 countries placed the UK alongside Canada, South Africa, Indonesia, Argentina, Netherlands, the USA and Palestine as having clear national/provincial policies for supporting engagement with research, within a growing trend of attention being paid to engaged scholarship. While Hall et al. provide extensive detail on community university research partnerships, in this chapter we focus specifically on the UK context as there are broader lessons to be drawn from this national experience.

A brief history of public engagement in the UK

Prior to the early 2000s, the UK's tradition of 'public understanding of science' had been framed around the need for scientists to communicate their work better and to promote understanding within the wider world. However, from the turn of the new century this tradition came under challenge, bringing an imperative to move beyond 'understanding' to 'engagement', with an emphasis on dialogue and mutuality. There were some significant steps along the way which helped this shift.

In February 2000, a government report (Select Committee on Science and Technology, Third Report, https://publications.parliament.uk/pa/ld199900/ldse lect/ldsctech/38/3802.htm) explored the relationship between science and society. Addressing issues of public confidence following the crisis caused by Bovine Spongiform Encephalopathy (BSE) – a high-profile public health scare – and rapid scientific advances (for example, in biotechnology and information technology), the Report identified 'a new mood for dialogue'. The numerous recommendations arising included 'that direct dialogue with the public should move from being an optional add-on to science-based policy making and to the activities of research organisations and learned institutions and should become a normal and integral part of the process' (Select Committee on Science and Technology, 2000: Recommendation 1, paragraph 5.48).

Despite this policy-level declaration, the academy was not necessarily prepared or equipped to engage effectively. This was evidenced by a significant Royal Society Wellcome Trust Survey (2006) into science communication, which revealed a problem with the prevailing culture in that 'many scientists see the main reason for engaging with the public as the need to 'educate' them rather than to debate, listen and learn as part of a genuine dialogue' (2006:14). It articulated a common complaint made of scientists that the public were regarded as a problem to be solved, rather than potential contributors to problem solving. Alongside this perception, academics were concerned that public engagement was a distraction from research (as we mentioned also in Chapter 5), rather than a potentially constructive contribution, and feared reputational damage if they were to spend more time on it.

A *Joint Statement on Impact* (Higher Education Funding Council for England, Research Councils UK and Universities UK, 2008: 01) sought to address these difficulties and declared a commitment to 'continue embedding throughout the research base a culture in which excellent research departments consistently engage with business, the public sector and civil society organisations and are more committed to carrying new ideas through to beneficial outcomes across the full range of their academic activity'. The *Statement* expressed a collective responsibility for achieving these outcomes, supported by effective and joined-up funding mechanisms, training/career development and management of research.

This new shared commitment by government, funders and universities to embedding a culture of engagement within academic activity was manifested in the creation, also in 2008, of the National Coordinating Centre for Public Engagement (NCCPE) and six Beacons (centres) for Public Engagement funded by Research Councils UK (RCUK). The NCCPE and the Beacon universities/consortia were tasked with galvanising culture change via pilot projects which would, in turn, influence the wider sector, transforming the UK's capacity for engaged research.

It is important to note, however, that while these policy developments, and the coining of 'public engagement' as a term, explicitly appeared in the 21st century, the idea behind them is not a new one within higher education. The medieval roots of our oldest universities, and the civic foundations of many subsequently, have ensured that a sense of public and social responsibility is woven into their fabric. In addressing the criticisms sometimes levelled at universities – that they are elitist and out of touch with public opinion – the opportunity to reframe long-standing civic or social responsibilities with a new and strategic approach to public engagement is attractive and powerful. Public engagement, done well, addresses directly the challenges of social responsibility, trust, relevance and accountability. Indeed, one of the original Beacon institutions, the University of Manchester, now aligns its public engagement activity within a core strategic commitment to 'social responsibility', which extends across its research and education remits (see Voice of Experience 6.1).

Working since 2008 with the Beacons and two subsequently funded groups, the 'Catalyst' and 'Catalyst Seed-Fund' institutions, the NCCPE has been inspiring and supporting the sector to 'create a culture … where public engagement is formalised and embedded as a valued and recognised activity for staff at all levels, and for students' (NCCPE, n.d.). Ten years on from the first 'early adopters', there are over 80 signatories (universities/research organisations) to the NCCPE's Manifesto for Public Engagement (declaring a strategic commitment to engage with the public and to celebrating and sharing public engagement activity), indicating that institutional aspirations, at least, in this direction are now widespread in the UK.

While substantial progress has been made over this time, the culture-change endeavour championed in the Manifesto remains a work in progress across the sector. Informed by the reflective report *The State of Play: Public Engagement with Research in UK Universities* (Research Councils UK and Wellcome Trust, 2016), further RCUK (now **UKRI**) funding has been invested to address remaining barriers and challenges. You can read more about these recent projects (and much else besides) on the NCCPE's website, cited in Further Reading at the end of the chapter. An example of these ideals put into practice is included as Voice of Experience 6.1.

Voice of Experience 6.1

Strategic journey: from Beacon to Social Responsibility

Public engagement at the University of Manchester has always beeh seen as some-thing the University should be doing as it is part of a community. It should be engaging and working with people, looking to share ideas, inspire informed dis-cussion, and involve people in its work.

Being a Beacon for Public Engagement raised the profile of engagement and brought it to the attention of senior strategic staff. In turn, they identified and created champi-ons to drive culture change and brought together different communities of practice, both within and outside the University, fostering new approaches as well as empowering people to engage.

Building on the work of the Beacon, a key element that has enabled the continued embedding of engagement has been its strategic positioning in the vision and gover-nance of the institution. In 2012, the University identified social responsibility as one of its three core goals, sitting equally alongside research and teaching. As a result, engagement now features in performance reviews at school, faculty and department level. It is regularly reported on within the governance structure and has a university-wide academic lead. It is formally recognised in University and faculty awards and in promotions criteria. It has also resulted in a more coordinated approach to community partnerships whether research-related, student volunteering or co-producing new galleries in the University's museum.

Other contributing elements include the continuous support of champions whether they are senior leaders, including the vice-chancellor, or individual practitioners. As the former Beacon project manager, my appointment in Social Responsibility has allowed the legacy and established communities of practice to continue. Additionally, engagement support and training are being embedded in staff and researcher devel-opment as well as in doctoral training colleges, upskilling staff and students.

It has been an exciting journey to date and one we are still making.

Suzanne Spicer, Social Responsibility Manager, University of Manchester

Public engagement perspectives

Within this changing research environment, the attitudes of researchers themselves have been shifting significantly within the last two decades, as evidenced by the 2015 survey, *Factors Affecting Public Engagement by Researchers* (https://wellcome. ac.uk/news/what-are-barriers-uk-researchers-engaging-public), which revisited the original 2006 survey. The 2015 results showed that researchers were now more motivated to do public engagement – with a high proportion understanding it as a two-way dialogue rather than one-way communication, and the majority agreeing it was their moral responsibility. (We will come back to this last point later.)

Interestingly (in view of the 'public understanding of science' roots of public engagement described above), researchers from the Humanities, Arts and Social Sciences (HASS) were shown to be more active and more confident than Science, Technology, Engineering, Mathematics and Medicine (STEMM) researchers; the survey showed only a small rise in STEMM activity since 2006 and only a minority feeling 'very' well equipped to undertake this work.

These disciplinary differences are referenced in the *State of Play Report*, noting that public engagement as a concept has 'become increasingly broad and encompassing, adopting a number of separate tracks such as Science Communication in STEM[M], Participatory Action Research in the Social Sciences and Patient and Public Involvement in the Health Sciences' (Research Councils UK and Wellcome Trust, 2016: 9). Drawing together, as it has, these different strands of tradition and practice, it is not surprising that public engagement can mean very different things to different people, be propelled by different motivations and drivers, and may look very different across a multiplicity of settings.

Researchers in the Social Sciences, whose work is typically seeking to change situations, reduce power imbalances or challenge dominant narratives, are likely to have a more sustained and deeper involvement with public engagement. Research in the Arts is routinely connected with artistic practice, exhibition and performance – and so may be by nature public-facing (but not necessarily 'engaging' in the two-way dialogic sense). STEMM researchers may be seeking public acceptance (to justify the use of public money), the management of risk, or greater understanding of 'user' or 'patient' experience. Jude Fransman (2018) highlights this complexity by mapping the various understandings of research engagement within several key policy domains and notes that:

> [T]he understandings of research engagement that emerge ... have evolved in a similar historical and geopolitical context, but through different approaches to thought and practice. Within each ... there are contrasting (and at times conflicting) interpretations of elements of research engagement including the 'whos' ... 'whys' ... 'wheres and whens' ... and the 'hows'. (2018: 202–203)

Thus, looking across the range of 'public engagement' activity, we can see a wealth of approaches and practices that are developing and shaping the UK engagement landscape. These may have begun separately within disciplines, but increasingly they are being brought together in new and collaborative engagement projects which cut across disciplinary divides to create dynamic opportunities. For example, the emerging notion of 'STEAM' (Science, Technology, Engineering, Arts and Mathematics – seeking to integrate art and design with STEMM disciplines to enable creative solutions and outputs) is bringing together artists and performers with science, medicine and health researchers (and sometimes health profession-als as well) to collaborate on public engagement. A prominent example is the 2014 Engage Award-winning 'danceroom Spectroscopy (dS)' (University of West of England and University of Bristol, www.publicengagement.ac.uk/case-studies/danceroom-spectroscopy-ds), which sought to make cutting-edge atomic and molecular research accessible via visual, sonic and choreographic ideas, using 'art as a powerful tool for communicating and immersing the public in complexity' (see *Key lessons learnt* on webpage).

What is interesting about the 'danceroom Spectroscopy' work, as is often the case with other collaborative work, is that by aiming to perform in 'a 360-degree projection dome', it created a new problem of scale, which then was solved by computing researchers. The case shows how 'a project that began to explore differ-ent ways to express science to the general public, ended up solving new technolog-ical problems that led to further research in order to perform in different spaces'.

Bringing together different practices and approaches can be fertile ground, not only to develop innovative engagement, but for the opportunity afforded to the different 'engagers' to learn from each other, expand their own engage-ment vocabulary and take new directions. When academic researchers collabo-rate with those outside their field or beyond academia (which is increasingly common in the current academic climate where greater emphasis is being placed on co-production), engagement practice can be enhanced as partners bring new approaches to the table. For doctoral and postdoctoral researchers, this is exciting territory to work in, as illustrated by the case in the Information Box 6.1.

Information Box 6.1

Living with dementia: ordinary lives, inspirational voices

Health Sciences researchers at the University of Southampton (including doctoral research-ers from the Alzheimer's Society Doctoral Training Centre) ran a project during 2016 and 2017 to provide opportunities for engagement between people with dementia, the researchers, artists and members of the general public. They aimed to demonstrate (to doctoral researchers, participants and wider audiences) the innovative methodological and theoretical approaches they were bringing to the emerging area of dementia research. They also aimed to facilitate public involvement via an arts project which would bring feed-back and advice to researchers (with the potential to direct future research as well as devel-oping engagement practice).

The project involved the creation of portraits which were constructed by the artist from words spoken by the people with dementia and/or their carers (via interviews led by the artist). This creative approach proved impactful:

When the artist interviewed people with dementia and their families, she took an open approach that foregrounded them as people or as a couple – 'tell us about yourselves'. When researchers produce information sheets that detail the …. problem under investigation, this sets a very different tone to interviews, where we ask people to focus on what is a problem, or what we think is a problem, however much we want the experience to be positive. The former was very refreshing to be part of as it enabled real joy and positivity to reign, and this then came across in the portraits. This was great learning for us as researchers in terms of how to promote positive engagement in research when working with people with dementia and their families. (Extract from the Final (internal) Report to Funder)

The resulting eight portraits were then shared with the people with dementia and their families/carers, and an individual copy was gifted to each of the 'sitters'. The full set of portraits was also exhibited publicly in several venues between July and October 2017. The responses and feedback gathered from the families and the public audience was collected and evaluated. Analysis showed that the portraits were very well received across both audiences, as enlightening, inspiring and emotionally engaging; the portraits challenged common assumptions and inaccurate portrayals of those with dementia, as they revealed the whole person. The comments below from Project Lead Tula Brannely (extracted from the Report to Funder) show the effectiveness of this creative approach to engagement, blending research with artistic practice:

This is the first time I have led an arts project and have found the process enlightening and interesting to work with people with dementia and families in a different way. It was a great opportunity for the artist, who received excellent feedback and exposure through doing the project. The PhD students were wowed by the different approach that the project took and the impact it had on the people with dementia and their families. The exhibition opening at the library was a very intense emotional time for everyone who had been involved, not least as there were people who had their portraits done who could not join us. … I expect to adopt similar approaches with other groups in the future, particularly when researching topics that are potentially emotive.

(For more visit http://generic.wordpress.soton.ac.uk/livingwithdementia/)

Public engagement and the personal response

Earlier in this chapter, we noted that most researchers surveyed in 2015 agreed that engaging with the public was their moral responsibility; perhaps this is not surprising as many in academia are inspired by wanting to make a difference in the world. This feeling of accountability (at a personal level, or perhaps on behalf of a funder or organisation) is one of many motivations for engaging. Sophie Duncan and Paul Manners (www.publicengagement.ac.uk/do-engagement/quality-engagement/purpose) propose six categories of purpose, which are helpful to summarise here:

- **Sharing what we do** – inspiring and informing to build understanding and stimulate curiosity in others. An important part of the engagement landscape (the link back to 'public understanding') is clear where engagement and 'outreach' (more usually linked to Widening Participation, that is reaching out to pupils from under-represented backgrounds, and recruitment) intersect – often very fruitfully.
- **Learning from others** – consulting to create research that is sensitive to and informed by how others make sense of the world.
- **Doing research/creating knowledge together** – research that builds and benefits from networks and expertise outside Higher Education and enhances the skills of all collaborators.
- **Influencing others** – wanting to have an impact on skills, behaviour, opportunity and community/social cohesion.
- **Responding** – to things that really matter to the public, drawing on their expertise/experience.
- **Applying knowledge together** – to ensure as many people as possible experience tangible/practical benefits from research.

Consideration of these various purposes and how they may connect with personal motivations and values will help you with planning for research engagement. Each different purpose will shape who to engage with, when to engage, what kind of engagement to undertake, and so on. For doctoral candidature, this might involve considering whether it is desirable (and possible) to weave public engagement into the research process to have a direct influence on the thesis and, if so, exploring what this would look like/entail. Alternatively, it might be that motivations are linked directly to the developmental benefits of engagement (broadening horizons, learning from others, getting out of the lab/office, a positive distraction!). As engagement is a dynamic process, it is also possible (perhaps even likely) that motivations and drivers will change and develop throughout a researcher's project/candidature. This is illustrated by the example in Information Box 6.2.

Information Box 6.2

The Beach Hut Brigade

In October 2017 doctoral researchers at the University of Southampton secured development seed-funding for a one-year project to enhance their own engagement practice as a large interdisciplinary group. Organising themselves to work together across disciplines, they designed activities which would 'capture the diversity of the coastline in one exhibit' in order to 'start new conversations and share knowledge about world-leading coastal research conducted across multiple disciplines and faculties'. Project lead Sien Van der Plank reflects on her own motivations and experiences:

In the earlier years of my PhD, the public engagement activity really helped with learning to verbalise (and, therefore, be clearer in) what the focus of my research was. Secondary school students especially can be quite sharp in their questioning of 'what you do', but without the pressure that a PhD student might feel when being asked similar questions by academics. Because the Beach Hut Brigade and its focus is more broadly on the coast, public engagement has allowed me to continually reflect about where my work fits in a broader context and in the 'real world'. I realised, for example, that coastal flood risk management isn't the only sector to desire more funding, that there are other coastal issues with an equally real need for focus and funding.

All of that said, I definitely did originally join the public engagement groups at the University (originally the Bioenergy group) to meet people at the University, to 'give back' to the UK (from where my funding has come, yet it is not where I am from), to share my enthusiasm for research and knowledge-building, to get out of the University and meet the public beyond the University...

Similar sentiments are expressed by other Beach Hut Brigade researchers:

Sharing my research with the public is one of the pillars of my motivation for (1) improving myself in the research field and (2) enhancing the outcome of my PhD. (Quotation cited in the Final (internal) Report for Funder)

As the project progressed, the team used their experiences to encourage and inspire others via a 'Hands-on Your PhD' workshop at the Festival of Doctoral Research:

Drawing your PhD helps you have a more/different schematic view of your project and how to make it understandable to a public who is not related to your topic. (Workshop participant cited in the Final Report for Funder)

Thus, while reaching 'public' audiences was the primary focus for the engagement work, it is notable that in planning and carrying out this project, the Beach Hut Brigade also placed considerable importance on informing and inspiring their own research community. And they clearly had a positive impact on academic colleagues as well:

I would be happy to consider including [the Beach Hut Brigade] in 'pathways to impact' in a grant. (Academic staff quotation cited in the Final Report for Funder)

The Beach Hut Brigade experience shows that public engagement can:

- Accommodate and shape a range of motivations, drivers and values – both 'personal/individual' and 'collective'
- Be fruitful at both an individual and collective level
- Bring clarity, contribute to learning and shape thinking (for the researcher, for the team, as well as for the 'public')
- Catalyse/galvanise collaborative work
- Model good practice to senior colleagues/leaders.

Doctoral Researchers of the Southampton Coastal Group

Public engagement and the doctoral thesis

Considering that early-career researchers (including those at the doctoral stage) are often the ones making public engagement happen on the ground, perhaps directed by, or on behalf of, their supervisors and PIs, it is worth exploring the extent to which doctoral candidature and its primary output – the thesis – are being influenced by, and may benefit from, these activities.

We have already seen how research funders have been influential in the development of public engagement as a concept and its emergence as a priority within the research landscape over the last decade or so. At doctoral level, its importance is signalled clearly within the Research Councils UK's *Statement of Expectations for Doctoral Training* (2016), which states that researchers 'should ... develop an understanding of the potential impact of their research on society' and specifically, that:

> Students should be encouraged to consider the broad context of their research area, particularly in reference to societal and ethical issues, and the importance of engaging the public with research. Learning and training opportunities should be provided to help develop their public engagement skills.

There is now a routine expectation that doctoral researchers will be trained in engagement and have opportunities to practise their skills. Of course, researchers do not need to use their own specific research to develop these skills, and it is perhaps more likely that early-stage researchers will be engaging on behalf of their group, supervisor or larger project. However, either way, one might expect these formative experiences to influence the doctoral path in some way.

There is also evidence that institutions are responding more formally to expectations of demonstrable engagement and impact within doctoral research, beyond the provision of training and practice opportunities. University College London (UCL), as part of its Doctoral Education Strategy, promotes the inclusion of an 'impact statement' in every doctoral thesis, which must describe 'how the expertise, knowledge, analysis, discovery or insight presented in your thesis could be put to a beneficial use'. The scope for where and how it may be brought about is encouragingly broad, incorporating journals, specialist or mainstream media, commercial- or social-enterprise, engaging with policy makers or with practitioners, academic and non-academic collaboration, and public engagement.

This feels like a **game-changer**: with a clear institutional requirement for all doctoral researchers to consider and document (as part of their assessed output, the thesis) how their research can make a difference and, within that requirement, drawing their attention to public engagement as one of the potential routes for making that difference. While the UCL requirement is for a statement within the thesis, there are already instances of a whole chapter being included, as with Matt Posner's story in Voice of Experience 6.2.

Voice of Experience 6.2

My unexpected thesis chapter

My thesis chapter on public engagement with research (PER) came about timidly. I had been heavily engaged in PER initiatives throughout my doctoral studies, using my research as a springboard for engagement. My PER projects were defined early on as a two-way discourse, motivated by having interaction and listening as a core element of the engagement exercise, with the aim to achieve mutual benefits. I had written extensively in conference proceedings for the optics and photonics community during my PhD, but would this fit into the narrative of a thesis?

From early on, my parents and partner queried if I would include my effort into my thesis. My PER peers and mentor were curious, but uncertain, about my research project. I floated the idea past my supervisors, and it was met with surprise, but not rejection, and I took that as encouragement. An outline began to form, which was debated at length. In one of my final PhD thesis meetings, I expressed doubt to my supervisors. They pushed back with encouragement, and I summarised four years of work and engagement material into a chapter for my thesis.

The chapter was discussed at my viva. My examiners appreciated the effort that had been done in conjunction with my research, but the legitimacy of the chapter in the thematic of my thesis was debated. I argued that this was an integral part of my research work. By traditional academic metrics, I was successful with papers, grants, awards and visibility. I had recorded methods and evidence of impact on the audiences and the development of translational skills for me, which, crucially, made the chapter about the exploration of public engagement with research activities and was a contribution to the novel and growing literature on the subject matter. Crucially, the chapter did not cause a perceived loss of value to my research and it was accepted.

The reaction of the community has been overwhelmingly positive since. I hope that my work will add to the literature on the framework for delivering and assessing research-inspired activities for engaging with the public.

Dr Matt Posner, University of Southampton

Going even further, there is a bolder vision for the doctorate of the future. Rick Holliman (Professor of Engaged Research at the Open University), in his 2013 blog-post (www.publicengagement.ac.uk/whats-new/blog/engaging-thesis, accessed 14 December 2018), projects ahead 20 years to consider what a truly 'engaged thesis' might look like in 2033. He proposes that engagement will be threaded through the entire doctoral process and not just an element included in the thesis submitted at completion. Thus, the 'dimensions of public engagement' will be considered from the earliest research proposal stage and, Holliman suggests, in terms of six Ps (which are paraphrased here):

- *People* – who should be engaging with this research?
- *Purposes* – who is being consulted with, with what aims and objectives?
- *Processes* – how and when are the relevant publics involved meaningfully?
- *Participation* – how will the participation of publics, researchers and supervisory teams be measured and explored?
- *Performance* – how will the quality of the engagement process be measured to inform future work?
- *Politics* – how will knowledge of the wider context for engaged research, and the localised political context of the publics involved, be demonstrated?

Continuing this **root and branch approach**, the supervisory team will include a member of the 'public' likely to be affected by the research, the thesis will include a report on how the six Ps outlined in the proposal have been addressed, and the examination panel will include a representative of the 'public' affected by the research, who will make a judgement alongside academic peers on the quality of the engaged research. This takes the concepts of co-design, co-production, mutual engagement and respect far beyond the borders of the academy and traditional notions about the thesis – its nature, purpose and audience. Radical indeed! Or simply a glimpse into the future?

Now, though, let us return to the present and consider how public engagement is being professionalised.

Professionalising public engagement

The recent proliferation of 'Public Engagement Professional (PEP)' roles in universities and research organisations, such as Public Engagement Officers, Professors of Science Communication, and so on, is notable and testimony to the emphasis now placed on these activities within the sector. Admittedly, a permanent contract in this sphere is not yet commonplace (particularly in academic-related or professional service roles), with structures generally tending towards the short-term and exploratory. However, sector-led interventions are galvanising momentum and opening opportunities for current and future generations of researchers. The NCCPE has trained several cohorts of staff specialising in supporting activity in this area since 2015 through its Engage Academy, and is also facilitating peer-to-peer support via a recently introduced PEP Network. They are also leading on collaborative development of a framework for 'public engagement professional skills, including exploring accreditation and recognition. An additional 'Engage Researchers Academy' was introduced in 2018, providing professional development for researchers to 'realise their potential for impact'.

These developments are bringing exciting opportunities for doctoral and post-doctoral researchers with a passion for public engagement and who are looking to establish their careers in this area.

Summary: what can we learn from public engagement?

The NCCPE claims there is 'compelling evidence that public engagement is critical to a healthy higher education institution', helping universities and research organisations to demonstrate accountability, to embody their values and purpose, to engender trust and demonstrate relevance. Public engagement also challenges the orthodoxy of institutional structural support, as the culture-change endeavours across the UK sector have shown. This activity does need time, training, encouragement and opportunity, although plenty of researchers go 'under the radar' (discussed further in Chapter 10) where formal or structured opportunities are not forthcoming. It requires policy and strategic support – if not nationally, then institutionally. Committed heads of department and individual supervisors and managers/PIs can build engagement into the research culture and projects of their teams, but overarching encouragement, connectivity, support and recognition at the institutional level will help with the sharing, development and sustainability of engagement practice (as raised in Chapter 4). One message to researchers is that they can lobby key people in their institutions in these areas and demonstrate, by their actions, the benefits of public engagement.

Undoubtedly public engagement affords benefits to individual researchers who can cultivate a useful set of skills and behaviours through their involvement (for example, see the Public Engagement Lens of the Vitae Researcher Development Framework, and Chapters 4 and 5). It can help to focus the nature and direction of research activity, test perceptions and opinions (those of the researcher and the 'public') and help to form an evidence base derived from evaluation information and data (formative and/or summative depending on the nature of the engagement). It can also be a channel for researchers to embody their own personal values and sense of purpose, as the examples in this chapter have demonstrated.

Public engagement also presents new challenges and implications. At an institutional level, it requires universities to become more porous, enabling an easier two-way flow of ideas, knowledge and people. For their engagement efforts to be effective and worthwhile, researchers too must open themselves up to listen and receive the ideas, opinions and suggestions of those beyond the academy, in some instances going even further to share the research process itself, that is, to engage in the co-production of research.

This work requires a degree of humility, to appreciate that 'non-academics' have useful and important knowledge and experience to contribute. In her plenary presentation to the 2018 (NCCPE) Engage Conference, Jen Wallace (Carnegie UK Trust) reflected on this use of the word 'non', which locates people on the outside, independent from where the power lies. She asserted that, in this age of 'fake news' and mistrust of traditional expertise, old assumptions and certainties can no longer be relied upon. Citing a Carnegie UK Trust stakeholder survey which showed that trust in academia is high but the use of academic evidence is low, she suggested that academics may need to cede power – as people will value what they have been involved in: the co-creation of evidence in this context. Stepping beyond the academy into a different community in order to collaborate could well mean becoming a 'non' in that new setting.

Fulfilment of Rick Holliman's vision would require a similar mix of boldness and humility if academia were to take the uncomfortable step of sharing the doctoral process with those beyond the academy, permitting them to influence the doctorate and its outputs. Although, as more and more doctoral and early-career researchers embrace public engagement, perhaps the seeds of transformation are already being sown.

Further reading

Fransman, J. (2018) Charting a course to an emerging field of 'research engagement studies': a conceptual meta-synthesis. *Research for All*, 2(2), 18 July. (See also a blog about this article located at: www.publicengagement. ac.uk/whats-new/blog/finding-common-ground-defining-our-differences-useful-map-public-engagement)

Hall, B., Tandon, R. and Tremblay, C. (2015) *Strengthening Community University Research Partnerships: A Global Perspective*. Victoria: University of Victoria, PRIA, UNESCO.

Higher Education Funding Council for England, Research Councils UK and Universities UK (2008) *Joint Statement on Impact*. Located at: www.ukri.org/files/legacy/innovation/jointstatementimpact-pdf/

Jones, B., Thomas, R., Lewis, J., Thornton, J., Read, S.M. and Jones, I. (2017) Translation: from Bench to Brain – using the visual arts and metaphors to engage and educate. *Research for All*, 1(2), 17 July.

National Coordinating Centre for Public Engagement (n.d.) Website. www. publicengagement.ac.uk/. This website includes lots of advice, examples and the manifesto.

Research Councils UK (2016) *Statement of Expectations for Doctoral Training*. Retrieved from: www.ukri.org/files/legacy/skills/statementofexpectation-revisedseptember2016v2-pdf/

Research Councils UK and Wellcome Trust (2016) *The State of Play: Public Engagement with Research in UK Universities*. Retrieved from: www. publicengagement.ac.uk/sites/default/files/publication/state_of_play_final.pdf

Royal Society Wellcome Trust Survey (2006) *Factors Affecting Science Communication by Scientists and Engineers*. Retrieved from: https://royalsociety. org/~/media/Royal_Society_Content/policy/publications/2006/1111111395.pdf

Select Committee on Science and Technology (2000) *Third report: Science and Society*. Retrieved from: https://publications.parliament.uk/pa/ld199900/ldselect/ldsctech/38/3802.htm

University of West of England and University of Bristol (n.d.) 'danceroom Spectroscopy (ds S)'. Retrieved from www.publicengagement.ac.uk/case-studies/danceroom-spectroscopy-ds

Wellcome Trust et al. (2015) *Factors Affecting Public Engagement by Researchers*. Retrieved from: https://wellcome.ac.uk/news/what-are-barriers-uk-researchers-engaging-public

7

What can we learn from doctoral training partnerships (DTPs) and knowledge transfer partnerships (KTPs)?

In this chapter we invite you to explore:

- Doctoral Training Partnerships (DTPs) and similar schemes
- Knowledge Transfer Partnerships (KTPs)
- What can be learned from them for doctoral and postdoctoral researchers, academic staff and institutions
- How they currently benefit all stakeholders and their further potential

Doctoral Training Partnerships (DTPs) and Knowledge Transfer Partnerships (KTPs) have been unique responses in the UK research landscape, both generating a variety of activity and possibilities for doctoral and postdoctoral researchers as well as supervisors and PIs. While this chapter focuses on these specific UK examples, we believe there are parallels that can be drawn to inspire researchers more widely.

What are DTPs?

Doctoral Training Partnerships (DTPs), Doctoral Training Centres (DTCs) and Centres for Doctoral Training (CDTs) are recent phenomena in the UK. These terms describe organisations of disciplines or universities, usually externally funded, which exist to provide funding and training for doctoral researchers. These organisations, along with others, such as Innovative Training Networks

(ITN) and Industrial Doctorate Centres (IDC), are funded by national Research Councils and have been developed to support the training and skills needs of doctoral researchers. While each discipline area has created its own model, doctoral researchers are often trained either as a group or cohort consisting of several disciplines or sub-disciplines from several universities, and so to facilitate this, a number of the centres require universities to form consortia.

For the sake of simplicity for the discussion in this chapter, we use the acronym 'DTP' to refer to all the models above unless we need to refer to one specific model. It is worth noting that, until 2013, there was no standardisation of terminology between the various Research Councils in the UK, which led to some confusion.

All DTPs encourage or require collaboration, which may be across disciplines, as mentioned above, and/or with external bodies, and all provide collaboration and networking opportunities for funded doctoral researchers. The earliest form of collaborative training centres was created by the Engineering and Physical Sciences Research Council (EPSRC) in 2003 and 2004, followed in 2011 by the Economic and Social Research Council (ESRC) and subsequently by the other Research Councils.

Most DTPs are funded through a competitive process, which means that the universities involved must commit to providing specific training and development opportunities for doctoral researchers. They must then deliver on these commitments and are closely monitored by the funder to ensure that this happens. In the few cases where there is no competitive process, the Research Council allocates DTPs according to the level of research income they award to the institution, and a similar level of commitment to training is expected.

DTPs vary considerably in make-up and there is no typical cohort size. However, training will involve both research and transferable skills and can be delivered at both institutional and cross-institutional level. Most frequently it is a combination of the two. Typically, multi-institutional training takes the form of conference sessions or seminars around a theme, and the sharing of courses and staff expertise where possible. It is worth noting that within this model, the doctoral programmes remain based in the individual universities. They are not run by the DTP, even though there will often be cross-institutional supervision of individual doctoral researchers.

What are KTPs?

Knowledge Transfer Partnerships (KTPs) have a rather different focus in that they are a specific model of collaboration between a university and business (or not-for-profit organisation, for example, a charity or local government body). They have been helping businesses for the past 40 years to improve their competitiveness and productivity through the better use of knowledge, technology and skills while giving early-career/postdoctoral researchers (ECRs) the opportunity to work in collaboration across the partners. The UK's Knowledge Transfer Partnership scheme started out as the Teaching Company Scheme in 1975 and was established by the government to bring together industry and academia. This became the KTP scheme in 2003.

The overall aim of the scheme is to use the collaboration between universities and businesses or third sector organisations to foster innovation and increase productivity by embedding new knowledge and skills. This is achieved by employing an 'associate', who is a graduate or postgraduate or postdoc to work on a specific project supervised by academics and individuals within the business. The associate is employed by the university for the length of the project, which can be from one to three years, but works at the company. The associate runs the project, gaining first-hand knowledge of how the business works. The types of project vary considerably depending on the needs of the business. Projects can involve the development of products or services. Alternatively, they can be related to business or organisational improvements.

The common ground between DTPs and KTPs

Although DTPs and KTPs are very different, through the structures created and with the financial support of the funder, they both provide an environment which not only facilitates collaboration but ensures the development and transfer of good practice. In addition, they provide the range of opportunities for researchers to develop and extend the professional skill-sets discussed in Chapter 4, which are so useful for CVs. This positive environment has enabled the development of practices which are as relevant outside the UK as they are within it. There are other similar structures elsewhere, as demonstrated in the International Examples 7.1.

International Examples 7.1

Similar schemes outside the UK

Examples of schemes outside the UK that foster collaborative and interdisciplinary work include the following:

- Marie Sklodowska-Curie ITNs are funded through the EU's Research Framework programmes and exist across Europe.
- Europe also has the EUCOR network of universities encouraging interdisciplinarity and networking across members.
- In Australia, the Australian Technology Network of Universities runs an Industry Doctoral Training Centre (IDTC), which is an Australia-wide industry research training programme focused on providing solutions to real industry challenges. This programme combines cutting-edge theory and traditional master's and doctoral research training with the professional and technical skills required by industry, commercial organisations, government, research organisations and not-for-profit groups.
- In the USA, the National Science Foundation runs the Integrative Graduate Education and Research Traineeship (IGERT) programme, which provides interdisciplinary research training and encourages collaborative research.

What do DTPs do well?

The concept of collaboration is embedded into the structure of a DTP and is often a requirement of the funder. Most are formed by collaboration of some kind between a group of universities and/or between a university and external partners. Collaboration is written into training courses, while collaborative studentships are actively encouraged or mandated. This means that, rather than being extra-curricular, collaboration is regarded as the norm. The culture within a DTP therefore encourages and enables collaboration and collaborative activity.

A DTP also tends to comprise a defined group of people and place emphasis on cohort building. Indeed, DTPs often run cohort-building activities for the group as part of their training offering. This group is likely to be multi-disciplinary and/or multi-institutional, and as such is a natural ground for network building and collaboration. The cohort within a DTP provides a secure environment for initial forays into collaborative activity. While some research groups and labs in other institutions may have close-knit teams, the DTPs provide structured activity and design their programmes specifically to foster integration and collaboration. DTPs must be imaginative about the training they provide in order to secure funding. By offering access to what is in effect an additional level of training at a cross-disciplinary level, often involving external partners, these partnerships provide enhanced access to skills and training needed for effective collaboration.

Although this was not always the case, DTPs generally now have funding to cover activities as well as doctoral researcher fees and stipends. That money is often ring-fenced to be used for collaborative activity, examples of which include funding specific researcher-led projects or events, activities with external partners or networking conferences. DTPs therefore provide funding for collaboration, which, like the funding targeted at public engagement discussed in the previous chapter, means this activity is protected and encouraged.

Many DTPs actively seek researchers to work on collaborative doctoral projects. In some cases, external organisations, such as major museums and the British Library, run their own doctoral programmes for which prospective researchers can apply. In the UK, the Arts and Humanities Research Council funds Collaborative Doctoral Partnerships which enable organisations such as museums and archives to apply for a block of funding that they can use to fund doctoral researchers co-supervised by a member of staff at a university and by a member of staff at the organisation. Projects are either selected through an expression of interest call or designed and proffered by the organisation. Selected projects are advertised widely to potential doctoral researchers.

Although common in the Sciences, in the Arts and Humanities a model involving a doctoral researcher applying to carry out a pre-defined project is unusual. Instead, it is the norm for the researcher to design their own project and apply to an open competition to fund it. The government is encouraging the new model further by using the DTPs as a mechanism for distributing streams of funding designed to encourage knowledge exchange between business and academia. Thus, many DTPs in HASS areas are responding by running specifically collaborative studentship competitions. In the Sciences, the collaborative model has existed for longer and is an integral part of many DTPs. All DTPs are therefore encouraging doctoral researchers to engage with collaborative doctorates. The researchers themselves have found some benefits in this mode of study, as the Voices of Experience 7.1 and 7.2 demonstrate.

Voice of Experience 7.1

The benefits of being a DTC researcher

My PhD focused on whether, and why, natural sounds such as birdsong can help individuals recover from stress and mental fatigue. It was funded through a SE DTC CASE award, with the National Trust and Surrey Wildlife Trust as partners.

Collaborating with these organisations allowed me to gain expertise in the fields of ecology and conservation, and to integrate these with my existing knowledge of environmental psychology. As a result, I published several chapters of my PhD in high-quality, peer-reviewed journals. My research informed Public Relations strategies and campaigns developed by the external partners, and as such increased the impact of my research beyond academia by encouraging public engagement with nature.

All parties involved in my collaboration were extremely encouraging of the project, and the external partners made both financial and in-kind contributions (for example, expertise, supervision and access to resources). Since my research informed the communications strategies of my external partners, we needed to find a balance between conducting the research and publicising it, and this was achieved through consistent communication.

As a DTC-funded student, I took up other ESRC opportunities during my PhD, for example, a funded internship at the Cabinet Office. This further increased the impact of my research and allowed me to develop my networks within the public sector. I look back on my SE DTC studentship as an extremely rewarding experience. I was able to concentrate on producing high-quality research and felt both supported and challenged to develop new ways of thinking. This provided me with a strong foundation on which to develop my academic career.

Dr Eleanor Ratcliffe, Researcher in Environmental Psychology

DTPs also encourage collaboration through funding placements and internships with industry, government or not-for-profit organisations during the studentship. Some funders are sufficiently enlightened to provide extensions of time to the doctorate to encourage uptake as well as funding the researcher during this period. In the same way that it channels extra studentship funding, the UK government provides access to DTPs to specific opportunities for placements and internships. For example, the Professional Internships for PhD Students (PIPS) in the biosciences are a unique and essential part of the UK Biotechnology and Biological Sciences Research Council DTPs set up in 2012. These are built to enhance PhD students' employability and broaden their training. The internships are typically 12-weeks long in non-academic environments where the student undertakes activities not linked to their PhD research topic. PIPS internships are fully funded and have no academic credit.

Caroline Pope (2015) conducted a study exploring the benefits of doctoral internships in a non-academic setting, drawing on data from 65 doctoral researchers from the East of Scotland DTP1 who carried out an internship as part of their doctoral training. Her findings indicated that the doctoral researchers developed 'self-awareness and [the] ability to critically evaluate personal, social and professional capabilities, skills and attributes'. Sixty per cent of the researchers questioned rated their internship experience as 'very positive' and another 36.9% as 'somewhat positive'. She stated: 'Overall the data provides a "sneak preview" of the dynamic additional force that participating in an internship is creating within UK doctoral training'. You can read more about Caroline's experience in Voice of Experience 7.2.

Voice of Experience 7.2

The benefits of internships

Internships are helping some PhD students to further broaden their horizons, particularly in relation to identifying potential career paths, thinking about where their individual true passion lies, gaining relevant personal and professional development experience and developing the 'global perspectives'. All of these have the potential to lead to more fruitful future careers.

For a PhD researcher who might be joining a DTP, the good news is that doing an internship is a fantastic way to develop yourself alongside creating unique research knowledge for the thesis.

In setting up and running the BBSRC Professional Internships for PhD Students (PIPS) Scheme within the East of Scotland Bioscience DTP1 PhD training programme, I get our PhD researchers to arrange their own internships so that they can mould things to suit their unique developmental needs. This is important because the BBSRC Internships must be unrelated to the PhD students' doctoral research topic.

It was exciting to find in my research study that there are lots of exciting benefits of professional internships matching personal career aspirations. PhD researchers discovered the great diversity of sectors and employers beyond the University. This suitably mirrors the multitude of career paths that exist for bioscientists.

By bringing their curiosity and imagination to shaping internship activities, PhD researchers are encouraging innovation and creativity in the workplace.

While carrying out their internship, the challenges encountered created unexpected learning for some. For example, one stated: 'I found it challenging to change the way I thought from a scientific/research view to a government policy making view'.

PhD students put their internship learning into effect when back doing their academic doctoral research role. Many were aware of noticeable changes in their confidence interacting with different people and in different work situations (77%). Others said that they were more open to new ideas and activities (62%). Half said they noticed a change in their confidence conducting their PhD research, and were managing their PhD project and time better.

For someone who has no experience of setting up a doctoral internship scheme within their PhD training programme, it can be confusing managing the expectations of employers, PhD students, PhD supervisors and universities. My advice is to start by putting in place a clear internship approval process that includes offering supportive feedback on internship plans. This maximises the chance of success. It is rewarding that, to date, 161 East of Scotland PhD researchers have completed high-quality internships with employers from 17 countries globally, and many have received job offers as a result.

Dr Caroline Pope, EAST of Scotland Doctoral Training Partnership

DTPs are also increasingly acting as brokers for collaboration, facilitating a relationship between their doctoral researchers and external organisations. Many (if not all) DTPs will have signed up external partners who have agreed to play a specific role in the DTP. That role will vary according to the needs and resources of the partner. It may be strategic or advisory, it may relate to training and skills development or it may be that the partner has agreed to provide internship projects. The DTP liaises with the doctoral researchers and the partners to encourage and facilitate the internship.

At the core of several DTPs is an existing university collaboration or consortium, for example, The White Rose Consortium of Leeds, Sheffield and York. This means that, in addition to those within the funded studentship programmes, there are other opportunities for doctoral and early-career researchers to collaborate across the three universities. The White Rose Collaboration Fund and Student Networks are great examples of good practice, supporting emerging, collaborative activities across the three partner universities, particularly encouraging activities which involve early-career researchers. You can find out more about this in Information Box 7.1.

Information Box 7.1

White Rose University Consortium Collaboration Fund

Since 1997, the Universities of Leeds, Sheffield and York have built on their individual strengths by collaborating through the White Rose University Consortium to add value from partnership activity in research, enterprise, innovation and learning and teaching. Working with a range of partners from the private and public sector, both in the UK and overseas, projects to the value of over £180 million have been secured by the universities.

One of the key tools used to encourage collaboration is the White Rose Collaboration Fund. This is a small pot of money of up to £11,000 awarded through a competitive process for projects that involve a minimum of six academics (two from each of the three White Rose universities). The Fund supports research projects that have the potential to lead to larger, more strategic initiatives and that may develop national and international linkages. A specific focus is the active involvement of early-career researchers in order to encourage an understanding and direct experience of how working collaboratively across the three universities will add significant value.

Many projects are led by early-career researchers who understand the need to secure external funding and acquire evidence of leadership for promotion opportunities. Support by senior colleagues is integral to the projects and there is a career development emphasis on communication skills, project management and experience of collectively writing external funding applications.

Between 2012 and 2015, 32 projects were funded to a value of £265,000, which went on to secure an impressive £23.5 million in external investment.

(Continued)

Examples

Below are three examples of the projects that the White Rose University Consortium has funded and some of their thoughts on the initiative.

Dr Zoe Darwin, School of Healthcare, University of Leeds

Project: Identifying and managing perinatal mental health in male partners using the Born and Bred in Yorkshire (BaBY) cohort

Zoe was an early-career researcher employed on a time-limited contract. She led the project team of 10 academics that included three professors and set up a group of key public and patient stakeholders. The project convened a one-day national symposium on gender, perinatal mental health and psychosocial aspects of reproduction, with researchers, clinical practitioners and community organisations across England. This bringing together of expertise strengthened the analysis and interpretation of their qualitative data and offered alternative perspectives on fathers and perinatal mental health.

Zoe was promoted to Lecturer in January 2017, published an article in *BMC Pregnancy and Childbirth* (H index = 90) and the *Journal of Health Visiting*, was invited to be a panel member for a national NSPCC project on gender and prevention of abuse, and presented at City University too. In Zoe's words:

> There is so much happening in the area of perinatal mental health and partners now and this funding has been a game-changer, enabling us to begin conducting research in this area. It's been such a positive experience for me, and I've directed a few people to the scheme. (Dr Zoe Darwin, University of Leeds)

Dr Kate Giles, Department of Archaeology, University of York

Project: York travel and transport in the Country House

Although led by a senior academic, this project was structured to create real-time opportunities for early-career researchers to work with curators from the Yorkshire Country House Partnership (YCHP). PhD students and ECRs were challenged to think creatively about the role of the country house in pioneering cutting-edge transport technologies and to explore the movement of goods and ideas in addition to people.

Three workshops were hosted by YCHP houses (Castle Howard, Kiplin Hall and Sewerby Hall) and 'Micro projects' were undertaken by Curators and PhDs/ECRs working together in Brodsworth Hall, Kiplin Hall and the National Railway Museum. Nine new papers were presented by ECRs at the Plenary Conference. An additional activity saw the creation of a virtual model of the Canaletto Room at Castle Howard as part of an 'Immersive Experience'.

> Reflecting back, it is very interesting how our activities have impacted way beyond our initial vision for the collaboration, not just within the Universities and houses, but also intellectually, in getting us thinking in different ways about future collaborative research and economic benefit around Immersive Experiences in the Country House. (Dr Kate Giles, University of York)

Dr Scott Lavery, Department of Politics, University of Sheffield

Project: Britain and Europe – the political economy of 'Brexit'

As an early-career academic lead, Scott Lavery benefited immeasurably from running this project. He organised four workshops and built a wide network with academics from across the UK. He was invited to disseminate research findings at the University of Oxford, to an ESRC workshop hosted at the Foundation of European Progressive Studies (FEPS) in Brussels, and to the University of Sussex politics department. He successfully secured a Leverhulme Early Career Fellowship and was appointed to a lecturership position at the Department of Politics at Sheffield. Outputs were many, including seven SPERI blogs (Sheffield Political Economy Research Institute); three SPERI papers, with one as a Special Issue to *New Political Economy*; and a paper, Finance Fragmented, in the *Journal of European Public Policy*, one of the top political science and EU studies journals.

> As a young academic, it's been great to be able to build a network in a manageable format, to make intellectual and professional connections, and to discuss intellectual issues. It's been hugely helpful. (Dr Scott Lavery, University of Sheffield)

What is unique to DTPs?

DTPs provide funding, training and collaborative opportunities in a supportive environment. As already highlighted, they have been established to foster a culture of collaboration and to encourage cooperative behaviours, be they across disciplines, universities or organisations. These opportunities are not exclusive to DTPs – all graduate colleges and schools will provide these in some form or other. However, what sets DTPs apart from those colleges and schools is the success with which they combine and emphasise these important elements, and importantly provide funding to facilitate collaborative opportunities, such as DTP-supported industrial placements and internships. The value of such opportunities for the researcher can be considerable, as illustrated in Voice of Experience 7.3.

Voice of Experience 7.3

Would I recommend an internship? Yes, I would!

Around halfway through my three-year PhD programme in health psychology, I undertook a six-month internship with Public Health England's Behavioural Insights Team (PHE BIT), which I was eligible for as a Research Council-funded student.

(Continued)

My PhD is exploring the use of antibiotics in farm animal medicine, focusing on vets' prescribing decisions in relation to long-term outcomes for animal and public health. I'm especially interested in understanding how psychology and social science can be applied to the big questions of public health, which also drives the work of PHE BIT.

This internship was therefore a great opportunity for me to gain experience in conducting and translating research outside academia. Although not directly relevant to my PhD topic, it was relevant to my broader interests, offering me a chance to develop in various ways:

- **Broaden my subject knowledge** – I worked on a wide range of public health projects.
- **Network with health professionals and researchers** – I enjoyed being part of a team of like-minded professionals, working with colleagues from the wider health and social care system, and presenting at conferences and workshops.
- **Understand the application of research in a policy environment** – I worked on exciting and high-profile research projects, some of which directly contributed to national public health policy goals, but I had to adapt to much shorter time frames.
- **Increase my confidence in my abilities as a researcher** – I realised that the skills and knowledge I possess as a PhD student made a valuable contribution to the team.

Would I recommend it?

Yes! Internships are not for everyone, but if you are considering a career outside academia, or are conducting research of relevance to policy makers or industry, such experience is invaluable. It also provided an intellectual break from my PhD, enabling me to return to university with new ideas and renewed enthusiasm, eager to push my research and career plans forward. Sometimes, a change really is as good as a rest!

Dr Sarah Golding, Researcher in Health Psychology

The importance of this combination is something that has been taken on board by other groups of universities, such as the Universities Alliance, which funds and runs its own Doctoral Training Alliance in order to give its doctoral researchers the benefits of a DTP-like environment. Several UK universities, for example Durham University, are extending the model and are now setting up Centres for Doctoral Training associated with the UK's Global Challenges Research Fund where supervisors or students have to collaborate with **Development Assistance Committee (DAC)**-supported countries with projects aimed at addressing global challenges.

What are the benefits of DTPs?

The benefits of DTPs are various, with lessons for doctoral and postdoctoral researchers (including those from overseas who would like to research in the UK), supervisors and PIs, as well as for collaborating institutions. We discuss each, briefly, in turn below.

Doctoral researchers

If you are still deciding where to do your doctorate, the obvious way to benefit from the good practice within DTPs is to apply to a university with a DTP in your discipline and then enter their studentship competition. Do be aware, though, that these are generally very competitive. If you do enter and are not successful, be reassured that all is not lost because many DTPs have 'associate' researchers who can benefit from DTP activities, such as training and conferences. It is always worth asking the university you are applying to whether associate researcher status is also available. Equally, if you are already doing a doctorate at a university with a DTP in your subject area, you can generally apply for funding, provided you have at least half your 'study time' left. If you are neither funded nor an associate, then watch for opportunities to engage with the DTP. Spaces on training courses and at conferences are often offered to non-DTP students, either free or for a small fee.

Early-career researchers

If you are an early-career researcher, you are not eligible to apply for a studentship, but you can take advantage of the culture created around the DTPs. We would also encourage you to take advantage of the subsidiary effects of the DTP. For example, your PI may be involved in the DTP as a supervisor in a training or management role, which, in turn, may open a few doors for you. If you are in an early-career academic role, you may have the opportunity to be more actively involved in the DTP from the other side and use the opportunity to network widely with university and external collaborators.

Supervisors and PIs

Where there are DTPs based within a university consortium, there are often DTP-type activities and support across that consortium as part of the commitment to collaboration between the universities. Because of that commitment, these activities will be designed to be collaborative or to promote collaboration or external engagement in some way (see the White Rose Consortium example above). DTPs also lead to more effective partnership working and to more opportunities for working with colleagues outside the university through cross-institutional supervision. Interestingly, a recent report (Budd et al., 2018) suggests that the first round of collaborative ESRC DTCs in fact had resulted in very little research collaboration between academics because of 'pre-existing cultural and competitive divisions' (see Chapter 10 on overcoming resistance).

Collaborating institutions

DTPs are aspirational and strategic. According to a Consortium DTC Director, the benefits are considered '...to be increased research potential across the three institutions, more research networks and more strategic research collaboration across the institutions' (quoted in Lunt et al., 2013). They have the potential to enhance the development of interdisciplinary cohorts, broadening the skills and knowledge of doctoral researchers beyond the boundaries of their doctorates. They also give the collaborating universities the opportunity to share best practice, training, expertise and resources.

In the UK, a funded DTP provides money for studentships, but also has a mark of quality that enables it to attract the best students. Additionally, there is a strong belief that the consortium has greater weight than the individual institutions, enabling it to attract external funding and external partners.

What are the benefits of KTPs?

KTPs encourage and foster two-way collaboration between universities and businesses. Businesses learn to work with universities and vice versa at an individual and institutional level. KTPs bring research skills and knowledge from the university through the associate and KTP supervisor to help the business or not-for-profit organisation solve a problem or address a challenge that will result in improving their productivity and profits. They give academics opportunities to observe and influence the practical application of their research, which in turn helps to increase the impact of their research. KTPs also offer opportunities to recent graduates to gain first-hand experience of working in a business or commercial organisation. The KTP scheme enables academics and researchers to work with external partners within an established framework supported by experienced KTP professionals. We highlight some of the main benefits for cohorts below.

Doctoral researchers and early-career researchers

There are opportunities for researchers after their doctorates have been completed to apply for an associate role on a project. This is an excellent way to gain first-hand experience of working in a business. Although a doctorate is not a requirement, it is certainly not a hindrance. Indeed, inside knowledge of the academy can often be an advantage when bridging between organisations.

Researchers gain experience of managing a project in a real-world setting with dedicated mentoring and the opportunity to gain further professional qualifications. Thus, the possibilities for enhancing your skill-set (as discussed in Chapter 4) are extensive. For those interested in a career in the commercial sector, many associates are offered a job with the company at the end of the project.

Once a project is agreed between the university and business, associate roles are advertised. Over 300 opportunities are advertised each year, which means that this is a considerable source of employment. Activity Box 7.1 provides weblinks to where these opportunities can be found.

Activity 7.1

Find out more about KTPs

Spend a few minutes searching the internet, following the suggested weblinks below, to find out more about KTPs.

1. Investigate the online resources provided by the UK Government at www.gov.uk/guidance/knowledge-transfer-partnerships-what-they-are-and-how-to-apply and by Innovate UK at https://ktn-uk.co.uk/programmes/knowledge-transfer-partnerships
2. What kind of jobs are available? https://info.ktponline.org.uk/action/search/partnership_vac.aspx
3. What kind of projects are supported? http://ktp.innovateuk.org/search.aspx
4. Is there support for KTPs (or an equivalent scheme) at your university?

Early-career academics (lecturers and assistant professors)

Universities employ KTP managers who are experts in Knowledge Exchange and in building partnerships. These people are likely to be found in your Business Development or Commercialisation Office. You can find out who your officers are either through your university website or through the government's KTP pages. It is useful to be alert to opportunities to engage with them, for instance through expert sessions or training courses. Look at any materials they produce and make sure you understand the scheme thoroughly.

Your KTP Office can help you to find a commercial partner from the organisations they already work with. They are also frequently approached by organisations who are looking for academic input to their business but do not know the right person to approach. However, many KTPs start with an existing relationship between the organisation and academic. The KTP experts then work with both parties to develop the relationship and the project. They also work closely with the government's local KTP advisors to ensure the project suits both parties and the government requirements. Although this can take a considerable time, if you are given support, such a project has a good chance of being funded.

Supervisors and PIs

A KTP is an excellent way for an academic to apply their expertise to real-world situations and produce high-quality research and publications while enhancing a relationship with an external partner and gaining new skills from working together. The parameters of the scheme are prescribed, but the assistance of the government's KTP advisors and the university KTP experts is invaluable to achieving a successful collaboration. This is also an excellent vehicle for you to develop opportunities for the researchers you may be supervising or managing. For instance, you could ask them to arrange a seminar with guest speakers from the partners.

Collaborating institutions

KTPs help to foster relationships between businesses and universities. Although individual projects can be small, the cumulative effect of several KTPs is considerable. They help to generate research revenue for universities as well as knowledge and skills to enhance research and teaching. There is also some evidence to suggest that they encourage innovation and entrepreneurship at the university. Commercial and not-for-profit organisations can increase innovation, productivity and performance by accessing academic knowledge and skills, embedding new expertise in the company in a very cost-effective way.

To sum up, if you are interested in a research experience, either as a doctoral or early-career researcher with built-in collaboration mechanisms, then it is worth looking at the opportunities to be found with DTPs and KTPs. These are both great examples of how to support and resource collaboration and collaborative activities. The support they provide is key to their success, and much can be learnt from them.

We close this chapter, and this part of the book, by reminding you that there are opportunities at all career stages. We invite you to consider where you might start to build collaborative relationships by looking at the weblinks included in this chapter and thinking about your own institution and research. Next, in Part III, we explore ways to help you progress confidently with collaborations and engaging others.

Further reading

Budd, R., O'Connell, C., Tinting, Y. and Ververi, O. (2018) *The DTC Effect: ESRC Doctoral Training Centres and the UK Social Science Landscape*. Liverpool: Liverpool Hope University Press.

Deem, R., Barnes, S. and Clarke, G. (2015) Social Science doctoral training policies and institutional responses: three narrative perspectives on recent developments in and consequences of the UK transition to collaborative doctoral training. In E. Reale and E. Primeri (eds), *Universities in Transition: Shifting Institutional and Organisational Boundaries*. Rotterdam: Sense, pp. 137–162.

Kitagawa, F. (2014) Collaborative Doctoral Programmes: employer engagement, knowledge mediation and skills for innovation. *Higher Education Quarterly*, 68(3): 328–347.

Lunt, I., McAlpine, L. and Mills, D. (2013) Lively bureaucracy? The ESRC's Doctoral Training Centres and UK universities. *Oxford Review of Education*, pp. 1–19.

MMAHMOODIAN Blog, *Marie Curie PhD, Advantages and Challenges...* Retrieved from: https://quicsblog.wordpress.com/2017/03/14/marie-curie-phd-advantages-and-challenges/

Pickerdon, C. (2018) *White Rose Collaboration Fund Outcomes for the White Rose Universities, Collaboration Fund Report* (July). Retrieved from: www.whiterose.ac.uk

Pope, C. (2015) Professional internships for PhD researchers: an integral part of doctoral training. Paper presented at the *Vitae Researcher Development International Conference, Occasional paper based on workshop C2*, 8–9 September, Manchester, UK (Vol. 3). Located at: www.vitae.ac.uk/events/past-events/vitae-researcher-development-international-conference-2016/vitae-occasional-papers. See also www.eastscotbiodtp.ac.uk/

Wynn, M. and Jones, P. (2017) Knowledge Transfer Partnerships and the entrepreneurial university. *Industry and Higher Education*, 31(4): 267–278.

PART III
Progressing with confidence

8

How can networks of trust be built and why do they matter?

Guest author: Erin Henslee

In this chapter we invite you to consider:

- The importance of trust to collaborations and engagement work
- How to build trust with your collaborating partners
- How to maintain and grow trusting relationships
- The role of reciprocity, 'giving and receiving', in a relationship
- Important matters that could undermine trust

The concept of creating effective working relationships and methods for this practice, as well as of building what we have called 'networks of trust', is grounded in the idea that if people trust you, they are more likely to work with (and for) you. Whether collaborating internally or more widely, all collaborators will be coming to the relationship with their own perspectives and priorities, all of which can affect how successful that collaboration or engagement will be.

This chapter delves into the reciprocal nature of research collaborations and examines other factors that may affect your network of trust, such as Intellectual Property. We will also address the difficult circumstances of closing an ineffective collaboration without interrupting the network of trust.

Starting with relationships

In earlier chapters we defined what was (and what was not) a true research collaboration. In this section we look at the core of what makes collaboration possible:

the people. Studies have shown that people desire to have strong relationships with people with whom they are working (Nielsen, 2004; Kang, 2013; Chakkol et al., 2017), going so far as to say that having a solid relationship grounded in trust is the most critical factor in collaborative success. You may be aware of the importance of trust already, through your relationship with your supervisor, line manager or PI. A study by Kay Guccione (2018) into doctoral researchers and their supervisors indicates not only that trust is a vital element in that relationship, but that supervisors can facilitate or build trust in their role as academic leaders. Trust, then, is central in answering the question we raised in Chapter 1, whether you are simply cooperating with your supervisor or PI, or if you are a developing a more collaborative relationship. While these relationships will form your immediate 'network of trust', you will need to build a wider network if you are undertaking collaborative or engagement work of any kind.

Taking the time to develop these relationships should be factored into your plans for building collaborative networks. This goes beyond getting to know someone through the normal work environment. Although you can interact successfully with people, by knowing their work styles, habits and motivations, trust comes from getting to know each other on a more personal level; indeed, this point is endorsed by various studies that have shown this human element to be vital in enhancing collaboration (Gratton and Erickson, 2007; Kang, 2013).

Knowing your value to a team

If you are a doctoral researcher or a new postdoctoral researcher, you may find that connections and camaraderie occur more organically in your closest surroundings at your institution among your peers. Making connections with those in your network that are senior to you may seem more challenging. It is important to remember that these senior colleagues, although more experienced, may still seek and prefer strong relationships with those with whom they work. It is also important to bear in mind the value you bring and contribute to a collaborative relationship is not dependent on your status, but the quality of your work and how you perform as a member of a team.

In Chapter 1, we indicated that engagement with your peers and colleagues was one of the elemental features of academic life and, in Chapter 2, we suggested that your immediate connections were an excellent place to begin, albeit in small ways. Here, we encourage you to actively seek connections with senior and junior scholars in your field. This is important because the wider your network is, the greater the chance that opportunities will arise. It pays to be a little creative in your search for connections. For example, you could search for the people who have recently been funded in your area or by contacting authors of papers you frequently cite or that you especially enjoy reading. Ideally, your network will then start to work for you, producing invitations to participate in departmental seminars or invited talks at conferences, and so on.

Relationships with industry

If you are involved with an industrial collaboration (or are thinking about this), you should note that while forming industry partnerships is one thing, nurturing them in the long term takes additional skill. Companies want to build trust with faculty members. In an interview with Venturewell, Anthony Boccanfuso, president of the University–Industry Demonstration Partnership (UIDP), states that faculty members should shift from **'transactional' relationships** with companies to 'strategic' ones, which require persistent, holistic engagement. 'Faculty members have deep relationships with companies because they support them along the continuum of engagement, not just in the sponsored research', he argues. For example, faculty members might use their resources to bolster the company's other pursuits at the university, such as introducing a capstone project (a short, two-semester research project) to the communications school or hosting a company's foreign delegation on campus. He continues: 'You want to be seen as a resource.'

Ultimately, collaborations and relationships are really all about making connections with people. In the words of Boccanfuso, in an interview (*University, meet Industry*), '[i]t's not companies and universities that make great relationships; it's the people at companies and the people at universities. If you have a strong industry–university partnership, there has to be a strong relationship between people' (Boccanfuso, 2018).

Keeping it personal

One important concept in establishing and being part of a network of trust is that its foundation is comprised of the people in that network. This does not mean you must have a deep, personal connection to everyone in your network, yet when you describe the people in your network, those descriptors include details beyond their professional CV. For example, you might describe the research area of someone you have met at a conference, but when you can describe them as someone who articulates well, who is enthusiastic about their field and is open to sharing ideas and collaborating, this is an indication that you have taken more than a passing interest in them. This signifies a relationship that goes beyond the superficial. Importantly, a non-superficial relationship also is dependent on how those in your network describe you, too. Reciprocity in depth of interest in each other is key. Top Tips 8.1 highlights the kinds of question to ask people in your network to reach deeper reciprocity, trust and engagement.

Top Tips 8.1

Getting to know your network

Some of the questions you can ask people in your network, to reach a deeper level of engagement, while also learning more about potential collaborative opportunities, include:

1. What excites you most about your project/research?
2. What are the biggest challenges to your work?
3. Where would you like to see yourself professionally in 5–10 years?
4. What are things you do to stay motivated?
5. Who has particularly impacted your career and in what way(s)?
6. If you could start your project over again, what would you change and why?
7. How might your work be relevant beyond your discipline?
8. What are the potential opportunities for your work?
9. What motivates you personally? How does that motivation impact your work?
10. What would be your ideal project and who would you like to work on it?

In an age of large, multi-institutional and global collaboration, one question that arises often is this: How do you establish a personal connection without meeting face to face? Today's digital communication offers a myriad of possibilities for staying connected remotely; however, remote connection can sometimes lead to the loss of the more subtle aspects of meaningful communication, which are often non-verbal or sensory, such as facial expressions, body language, hand gestures, even mode of dressing, etc. Also lost are the more social aspects of meetings, such as a pre-meeting coffee or tea accompanied by a quick chat about non-work-related topics, such as family, mutual friends, shared interests, and so on. All of these aspects of meeting bring the human element to our communications with others and need to be retained as far as possible to nurture the personal connection among collaborators.

For these reasons, where face-to-face meetings are not possible, it is important to choose an alternative mode of meeting that permits a degree of social interaction. Video-conferencing, for example, is a good alternative to face-to-face meeting as it provides the opportunities for all parties involved to interact socially, to gauge the facial expressions of others and to glean the non-spoken responses of others to what has been said or proposed.

It is also important to factor into allocated meeting times opportunity for social interaction, perhaps before or after the formal meeting, as this creates a space for individuals to get to know each other beyond the work context. For example, either virtually or in person, when building relationships with potential collaborators, you could spend this time learning more about the other areas your collaborators are working in, sharing yours as well. This gives you a broader perspective on your collaborators' time commitments and priorities, and vice versa. It may also introduce you to new connections, people and organisations that you were unaware of and that may be useful to your collaboration or engagement activity.

Taking time in this process ensures you are choosing the correct people for your collaboration. Building the relationship first will inform you about what the person is like to work with, where their priority areas of research and impact are, and if the rapport is not there, it offers a chance to walk away. There is a Dutch saying, attributed to Johan Thorbecke in the 19th century, that 'trust arrives on foot, but leaves on horseback'. This suggests that, although trust takes time to cultivate, it can be lost rather rapidly if you fail to work at maintaining the relationship, as we discuss below. Personal interactions and being curious about each other are vital to the relationships that make for successful collaborations and engagements, as we indicate in our Collaborative Code, presented in Chapter 1.

Giving the gift of time

Collaborative partners have to be able to work with each other in order for collaboration to be successful. Finding the time to develop sufficient rapport to foster a positive collaborative relationship can be challenging because it often requires an informal approach and therefore is not something tangible that you can include as a deliverable on a Gantt chart or explain in a performance review. When polled, doctoral researchers and early-career researchers (ECRs) at one of the author's institutions shared their strategies for finding the time to nurture and/or build rapport with colleagues and collaborative partners:

> 'I save networking emails for evening/weekends. I will often schedule them to go out the next business day in the morning, so I don't look like a crazy person, though.'

> 'I often have coffee with groups as opposed to individuals.'

'I will try and slot in chats before or after seminars.'

'I use social media and build it into my work. I am promoting my research and personal brand.'

The good news is that the commitment of time is in itself a tangible artefact you have created within your network. In a professional world where everyone is busy, those small gifts of time you can give to people will go a long way in building your side of that relationship. But how do you account for this time when it comes to items such as your performance reviews? Some of this can simply be reframing that time around a specific project or task. For example, one of your authors wrote in a current performance review: 'In the first six months I have focused my efforts in terms of getting to know my area/community through conversation with colleagues, seeking opportunities to assist colleagues in their work, and sharing my experience in public engagement and outreach as a resource when needed.'

Building trust during collaboration

Having spent time building a relationship, at what point is the network of trust (which we believe is essential in all collaborative relationships) established? First, let us address the notion of a 'network' of trust. This would include people you would recommend to others for collaborative purposes and hopefully would include those referring you onwards to other potential collaborators as well. This can also mean having a variety of people you can draw on to build a collaborative team for a specific project or topic. Although you may be the 'centre' of your network, any network will naturally contain interconnected members. Indeed, part of having an active network is creating more connections within and adding connections from external places. However, this should not be done arbitrarily. The idea underpinning this concept is that of trust. Therefore, these connections can be purposefully made knowing that those contributing to the new connection are trustworthy and reliable sources.

Establishing the working relationship

In this section we focus on how you establish trust within your collaborative teams and achieve the goal of establishing a reputation for yourself as recommendable and trustworthy. You want your name to be at the top of their list when your network connections create an opportunity that might fit you well.

As we emphasised in Chapter 2, it is sensible to start small with a new collaborative project and team. Consider it a test drive of the collaborative team. This will give all members on the team a lower stakes investment. That is, it will provide you with the opportunity to identify differing working habits and project management styles, as well as the chance to negotiate tasks and identify unique areas of strength of the team. There are a number of questions you should ask yourself about your collaborators at this point to help you gauge their suitability for your team: Do you trust them to follow through? What is their track record of delivery? Is everyone bringing equal value to the relationship? Is there potential in the ideas? How do you feel immediately before meeting with them – excited or unenthused? This final question is extremely important. If you feel unenthused at this early stage, how sustainable will your relationship with that person be when your collaboration encounters challenges and/or obstacles, as it invariably will?

If you have an existing network of people you are starting a collaborative project with, Activity 8.1 introduces a way you can initiate putting this idea into practice. This is also a good exercise if you are facilitating a networking event or if you are putting students in teams and need an exercise for them to create a team working 'contract'.

Activity 8.1

What are the attributes of your ideal team member?

Part 1

Have each person in your group list as many attributes they can of their ideal team member. Leave it open for everyone to interpret this in their own way. If doing this exercise in person, Post-it notes or note cards would work best for the next step. If doing this virtually, consider using a digital pin board or shared spreadsheet.

Part 2

Now, in discussion, organise that list into four categories:

- Hard skills/competencies
- Soft skills/competencies
- Behaviours/qualities
- Habits.

Hard skills and competencies would be items such as a specific programming skill, familiarity with a specific framework, writing or editing. Soft skills would be less tangible such as people skills or being a good communicator or being organised. Behaviours and/or

(Continued)

personal qualities are broader and can include items such as resilience or generosity. The fourth category, habits, would include the items you notice that people do, such as being punctual, responsive to emails, or that they bring snacks (this was an actual answer given in a workshop one of your author's ran – it was clearly an important team-building attribute).

Part 3

Provide time for personal reflection. Then, each member of the group should take a turn in describing which attributes they think they can best bring to the team, which they think they could develop further and which they have concerns about living up to. For example, you might be skilled in database management, but know you are not good at email communication.

This final element of the activity might be uncomfortable, but it affords a group the opportunity to consider what is important when working together and to be aware of what each person can contribute.

Continuous improvement

Building trust is an iterative process; it will grow as the interactions team members have with each other increase and as involvement in the collaborative or engagement work intensifies. It may take some time and several meetings or interactions before everyone is able to be as candid with each other as Part 3 of Activity 8.1 requires. Therefore, we also recommend that everyone is committed to building the relationship first, as these conversations become easier the more comfortable you are with each other. Having the opportunity to be open and honest with each other, especially about what your expectations are of the collaboration, of the team, and what you can and cannot contribute, is an implicit way to consider what 'trust' means. It is through the sharing of expectations and personal attributes, and even of potential vulnerability, that you can begin to place trust in one another. Further, encouraging the use of positive and inclusive language can be a powerful tool that enables the team to 'appreciate' each other and to recognise the range of positive attributes. Reflection Point 8.1 invites you to review your use of language.

Reflection Point 8.1

Words are powerful

We all take the words we use for granted – after all, we use them a lot. Sometimes, though, we can be unaware of the impact our words have on those around us. How positive, appreciative, inclusive or celebratory are the words you use?

Next time you write an email or are in a meeting, reflect on what you have written or what is being said by colleagues. Are there any words that seem negative or might engender an unenthusiastic, unhelpful or unhappy response? What alternative terms or phrases could be used to create a more positive effect? Changing negative phrases, such as 'no but...' into the more positive 'yes and...', is a good habit to acquire. We can change the discourse or 'stories' we tell by changing the words we use.

Negotiating the 'give and take' of relationships

The reciprocity, or levels of 'give and take', required at the beginning of new collaborative relationships can be difficult to navigate. It is possible, when working with senior colleagues, that you are asked to provide the groundwork side of the project, while they provide more of the oversight and ideas. Certainly, if you are new to an established collaborative group, you may find the need to 'prove yourself' as a reliable member. However, this is not, nor need it be, always the case. As we explored in Part I of the book, it is becoming more commonplace for doctoral and postdoctoral researchers to be the epicentre of collaborative projects and engagement work. If you are in this position, then you will need to draw on your people-management skills, which we explored in Chapter 4, remembering also the principles of 'compassion' and 'curiosity' in the Collaborative Code (see Chapter 1).

It may sound obvious but building trust early in a collaborative team can often be difficult if meetings are infrequent and while you are balancing effort for the team with your other obligations. In addition, you will all be developing an understanding about how best to make the collaboration work. However, there are some strategies that help to foster trust early on in a collaborative team. They include:

- **Negotiated, clear expectations**. Let your collaborators know your other obligations and the time you can afford to give to the project. If you cannot deliver everything, be honest about what you can do.
- **Transparency**. This can be achieved through simple email updates, using collaborative software or file sharing, and being open about problems or concerns. Everyone needs to feel included and informed.
- **Meeting deadlines**. Early collaborative projects fail when other obligations, such as teaching, primary research deliverables, or life's obligations, take precedence. If you need extensions, renegotiate as early as possible.
- **Follow-through and gratitude**. This goes beyond meeting deadlines. It includes actions such as sending the enquiry you said you would, thanking people for their time and giving feedback when requested, as well as thanking those for their feedback. Again, this contributes to feelings of inclusion and also of being valued and welcome in the team.

- **Allow time for personal development**. Try to incorporate ways in which your team can get to know one another and develop their personal relationships with each other. Additionally, devote project time to knowledge sharing and group learning based on the skills your team have identified.

Keep in mind, these are not just tips for you, but qualities to look for in your collaborators and collaborative teams. As a new PI, or leader of the collaborative team, much of the expectation management and organisation of meetings will be your responsibility. You may also have to follow up if members of the team fail to meet expectations.

Early problems can often arise due to a mismatch of expectations or communication breakdowns. If a relationship is growing into a collaboration, members of that collaboration should have open and frank discussions around the expectations of collaborative effort. Questions to ask yourself and your collaborative team are: What am I/are you expected to contribute? What do I/you expect to get out of this collaboration? What resources am I expected to contribute? What are our timelines for deliverables? A useful skill to employ in these circumstances is a facilitative rather than a direct form of questioning, a form of coaching technique. This is explored in greater depth in our sister volume in the series, *Success in Research: Mentoring to Empower Researchers* (Hopkins et al., 2020).

Put it in writing

These early discussions and negotiations can result in misunderstandings. These might include areas related to important aspects such as team-member accountability, authorship credit and data management. However, written agreements, or at least documentation of the agreed plan, can help prevent future misunderstandings and protect those less comfortable with confrontation.

Indeed, you may not be able to enter into any form of collaboration or engagement work without a written agreement or understanding, or, at least, a risk assessment. You may also be required to conduct a gender and/or environmental impact assessment. Therefore, you should check what requirements your institution and your collaborators' institutions have with regards to written agreements from the outset. There will be legal officers who can advise you on these matters, and it is best to consult them in the early stages to avoid potential problems. No matter how small your project is, you should always review the risks, the ethical and contractual matters, and do so by seeking the advice of experts in these matters. See Information Box 8.1, which is a checklist of the key areas of consideration.

Information Box 8.1

Items to consider that require written agreements

Here is a list of the areas that commonly require a written agreement:

- Authorship
- Intellectual Property
- Data management, sharing and ownership
- Funding arrangements
- Team or collaboration agreements (often needed for grant/bid proposals)
- Material Transfer Agreements
- Facility and equipment use
- Business agreements (such as liability in the event of problems)

By creating clear working guidelines that have been collaboratively agreed upon, it is less likely that you will encounter a breakdown in trust in your collaborative relationships.

Maintaining trust during collaboration

In preceding sections, we explored how to build trust with new acquaintances and then how to take some initial steps towards building trust within a team. However, once the team is working together, maintaining those relationships and continuing to strengthen the trust within the team is equally important. Of course, keeping to what was agreed upon in terms of work allocation, time-lines and outputs will be the primary driver of trust within a collaborative team. In addition to these, there are other strategies that you can deploy to make that connection deeper. Below, we highlight some key strategies that will enable your team to maintain and build upon the foundation of trust established.

Facilitate time for reflective practice. Give your team time to reflect on their activities. What is going well? What is not going well? What can be improved and what is out of the team's control? These questions should be raised regularly, at least in concert with the team's cadence in deliverables. For example, if a team meets weekly, having a review once a month would give four points of reference to reflect upon. If a team only meets once a month, you may want to reflect every other meeting, so that problems do not go unchecked for a long period. Regular, reflective practice will ensure problems are addressed quickly. It is also important that this reflective practice is collaborative, with everyone having an input, and should be documented in some way.

Change management. A general rule of planning is that the plan will have to change. Being transparent during change and having good change management strategies will keep trust going even if plans and agreements must be altered. Change is seldom easy, so addressing it collaboratively and as openly as possible will help maintain trust. However, remember that moments of uncertainty can also provide excellent opportunities for the team to be creative.

Allow time for personal team development. We mentioned this earlier in the team development phase but maintaining this as the team functions on a day-to-day basis is an important aspect of strengthening connections. If you are primarily working virtually, you should allow time for these types of team-building events within your team's in-person meeting spaces. Personal professional development plans, especially if beneficial to the team's goals, should be negotiated at the beginning, but could also evolve as the project develops. These opportunities should be equitably distributed.

Maintain good habits of communication and transparency. When first building your team, you may spend a lot of time and effort learning how to work with each other, the best modes of communication and how to keep regular logs of meetings and decisions. It is important to reiterate the importance of maintaining transparency, openness and good communication as you move forward and become more comfortable with one another.

Leadership style. If you are leading a collaboration or engagement, you should be aware of your leadership style and what impact that can have on the team, whether it is enabling or inhibiting in any way. Taking regular feedback from your colleagues is one way of reviewing your style. Further, we would strongly recommend undertaking training in this area. Leadership training is not just for senior staff; this is something that doctoral and postdoctoral researchers should engage in too – helping you to prepare for future roles.

Maintaining trust and saying no

As you can tell, building your network of trust is mostly paid for in the finite currency of time. You will not have time to build and maintain every relationship to the same degree of familiarity. You will, however, need to nurture them all – like tending plants in a garden. Some may just need occasional attention; others may need more effort. Professionally speaking, start with those relationships that are organic (naturally occurring and working well) and those directly related to your research or professional goals. As your network grows, you may find you will have to say 'no' more often than you are saying 'yes' to opportunities to collaborate or engage with your network. You must be strategic about when to say 'yes' and when to say 'no'. Saying 'no' is not easy and has the potential to undermine trust, so we consider difficult decision making next.

Take your time to respond

As your schedule fills up, be sure to give yourself time to make considered decisions. If a request is given in person, this can be particularly challenging. You could ask if you can have time to think about it and give a timeline for when you will give them answer. People are very accommodating if they know when to expect a response. During this time, you can assess your own time commitments, the merit of the idea and what impact it will have for you professionally. It may be an opportunity you cannot pass up, but you still must find the time and may have to re-negotiate other commitments.

Another conundrum occurs when the commitment requested is not, for you, worth the time it requires, yet the person making the request is someone you would really like (or need) to work with. You could spend time thinking creatively about how the project could be altered slightly so that it requires less of your time or produces greater value for you. There are generally creative solutions and compromises to be found. However, it may simply be something you have to say 'no' to, and there are ways you can do this without breaking a connection.

How to say 'no'

There are degrees of declining a request, which, if conveyed politely and with an explanation, should not undermine the level of trust you have established. Possible ways of saying 'no' include:

- **Saying a partial 'no'**. Perhaps you cannot do all that is asked, but you could contribute a smaller part. Be clear on what you can do and what you do not have time to do.
- **Saying 'no', for now**. Maybe the time just is not right, but it could be later. Give your collaborator a timeline for when you would be able to say 'yes'. This might not align with their needs, but it is way to stay on their radar for the project later.

- **Give feedback with a 'no'.** You must decline, but you have some ideas for the project you can share. This could even lead to an acknowledgement later.
- **Say 'no' and suggest someone else.** This is a real 'network in action' moment. Maybe you do not have time but know of others who might be interested. If the people do not know each other, offer to make those connections and follow up on that connection in a few weeks.
- **Say 'no' but explain that you cannot do the task justice.** Demonstrate that you value highly what has been suggested but your other obligations restrict you.

In Chapter 4, we give some tips (see Information Box 4.2) on how to deliver bad news sensitively. The method should be polite, yet firm, to ensure the other person understands why the answer is 'no' and that they are left with their dignity and integrity intact (as yours are too).

What happens after the collaboration is over?

You will most likely work with some of your collaborative partners more than once, but there are many instances, such as leaving academia, changing research paths or other developments in your career which preclude you from directly working with someone again. Without the need to work together, consistent contact can be hard to maintain among busy lives. A proven track record of trust built throughout the project should mean that there is at least a foundation to work on. You may wonder if a network of trust can include people you have not, or will not, work with. The short answer to this, is yes!

Maintain the relationship

In the first section, we stress the importance of personal connection. The personal aspect of the relationship does not go away when the project is done or after the connection has been established. Perhaps you might never collaborate with some of these people through research again, yet you will have established a good professional connection. Maintaining these connections is worthwhile because one never knows what they might lead to in the future. These are exactly the types of connection that could lead to the other types of collaboration we explore in Chapter 2, such as planning a seminar series or conference. Maintaining personal contact facilitates meaningful interaction and keeps you on their radar should a further opportunity arise. Again, the time investment of maintaining these connections pays for itself when your network starts 'working for you' – that is, when you receive invitations and offers to join in other people's projects. Consider Voice of Experience 8.1.

The lifelong importance of networks

We have so many connections in academic life. There are simply such a lot of lovely people to meet, work with, be friends with, support and be supported by. It is true that sometimes you lose connections with people because other parts of life take over, but that does not mean they are lost forever, even when the annual greetings cards stop coming. Two examples come to mind.

One occurred when I was due to attend a conference in a foreign land and remembered an old contact had moved there. I looked him up on Google and sent a message saying when I would be there, in case he might have the time and inclination to meet. He did; his and his family's hospitality was wonderful and was extended to a newer research colleague accompanying me; they found a mutually beneficial business interest; we three are all now in contact to pursue new interests.

Another occurred a few months after my first 'retirement': another conference attended because I was so bored with domesticity; another long-lost colleague encountered; an offer of another job, which in turn led to the challenge/contentment of a large book series.

A Professor Emerita

The impact of connection

These connections are important for many reasons beyond research collaborations. If you have worked with collaborators senior to you, for example, you could ask them to write references, letters of recommendation or statements of support for jobs and funding applications. Collaborators are also the foundation of your citation community.

Citations and sharing are easy-win ways you can keep connections and maintain trust. The foundation of trust will allow you (and those in your network) to use your online presence to help promote each other's work. This is where your time commitment in building and establishing trust starts to pay off. While you would not blithely share papers or articles from people you do not know well enough to trust their work, if you see a previous collaborator has put a blog post out, or published a new paper, you could quickly share this with your community knowing you are sharing quality pieces. In return, your collaborators are hopefully doing the same for you!

Top Tips 8.2

Staying connected

Here are some ideas for staying connected with people outside a direct collaborative project. You could:

1. Form writing groups (virtual or in-person).
2. Establish **peer review** groups for papers and proposals.
3. Share and cite each other's papers.
4. Forward opportunities you come across.
5. Send invitations for people to give a talk in your department.
6. Offer to give a talk in their department or organisation.
7. Organise conference and seminars and invite them to contribute to the programme.
8. Seek opportunities for the cross-discipline or cross-institution supervision of PGRs.

Trust fosters the best ideas

In closing this chapter, we reflect on why building trust matters. Being a part of a team and working together builds trust. When you trust the people you work with, you are building a relationship and a working environment in which people can get along, care for one another and generally feel welcome. Without trust, you may encounter resistance, which we explore in Chapter 10. Being part of a team built on trust will make you more daring because this kind of team encourages and supports the creativity, curiosity and constructivism that collaboration and engagement need. It is less likely that you will take as many intellectual risks when you are working alone; however, with the support of such a team, you have the freedom to approach challenges from different perspectives, take healthy risks and generate new ideas.

Further reading

Baldwin, R.G. and Chang, D.A. (2007) Collaborating to learn, learning to collaborate. *Peer Review*, 9(4). Retrieved from: www.aacu.org/publications-research/periodicals/collaborating-learn-learning-collaborate.

Boccanfuso, A.M., (2010) Why University–Industry Partnerships Matter. *Science Translational Medicine* 29 Sep 2010: 2(51). Retrieved from: https://stm.sciencemag.org/content/2/51/51cm25/tab-pdf

Boccanfuso, A.M., (2018) Interview with Venturewell. *University, Meet Industry: 4 Ways Faculty Can Make and Keep Strong Industry Partnerships* [see Maximizing Relationships with Industry Partners]. Webpage https://venturewell.org/industry-partnerships/

Chakkol, M., Finne, M. and Johnson, M. (2017) *Understanding the Psychology of Collaboration: What Makes an Effective Collaborator?* March. Retrieved from: www.instituteforcollaborativeworking.com/resources/documents/research_report_2017.pdf

Gratton, L. and Erickson, T.J. (2007) Eight ways to build collaborative teams. *Harvard Business Review*, November.

Guccione, K. (2018) *Trust Me! Building and Breaking Professional Trust in Doctoral Student–Supervisor Relationships.* Leadership Foundation for Higher Education. Retrieved from: www.lfhe.ac.uk/en/components/publication.cfm/SDP2016Sheffield

Hopkins, S., Brooks, S.A. and Yeung, A. (2020) *Success in Research: Mentoring to Empower Researchers.* London: SAGE.

Kang, H. (2013) *Improving Collaboration: Start with Relationships* [Web log post], 15 March. Retrieved from: https://blogs.cisco.com/collaboration/improving-collaboration-start-with-relationships-2

Kelly, M.J., Schaan, J. and Joncas, H. (2002) Managing alliance relationships: key challenges in the early stages of collaboration. *R&D Management*, 32: 11–22. doi:10.1111/1467-9310.00235

McCalman, J., Paton, R.A. and Siebert, S. (2015) *Change Management: A Guide to Effective Implementation* (4th edition). London: SAGE.

Nielsen, B. (2004) The role of trust in collaborative relationships: a multi-dimensional approach. *M@n@gement*, 7(3): 239–256. doi:10.3917/mana.073.0239.

9

How can you initiate collaboration and wider engagement?

In this chapter we invite you to consider:

- The benefits of being proactive
- Advice on planning your own collaborative activity
- Guidance on facilitating your own collaborative activity
- Practical, inexpensive and easy-to-run examples for collaboration and engagement
- Some of the challenges you might face
- Suggestions for addressing any potential challenges

While involvement in an existing collaborative or engagement activity or event might provide you with your first steps in this arena, you will want to progress to your creating your own events or activities. Indeed, the longer you remain within academia, the more likely it is that you will, and in our view should, be initiating this kind of activity as you will recognise the value and importance of collaboration and engagement for your career. In this chapter we explore ways in which to bring like-minded people together either to inspire and generate ideas for a specific project and activity, or to explore broader research synergies.

Benefits of initiating collaboration or engagement activities

Initiating an activity or new project is excellent experience and will help you to develop your skill-set further, especially in terms of organisation, management and leadership skills. Remember that real 'development' (or change in your behaviour) comes with honest self-reflection and feedback on your performance, so you will need to take a broad approach to initiating new projects if you wish to benefit professionally from such activities. New collaborative/engagement projects provide stimulation for discussion with your colleagues, supervisors, PIs and/or mentors. For researchers with experience in other sectors, for example, mature and part-time researchers as well as those undertaking **professional doctorates**, collaboration and/or engagement provide excellent opportunities to bring your existing skills into the academy and to enhance them further. For those without such experience, initiating and facilitating such activities will help you to enhance your knowledge, behaviours and skills and is an excellent way to raise your level of visibility among colleagues and external collaborators or potential collaborators. On a more mundane level, it gives you the opportunity to work with academic and professional services colleagues you are likely to encounter as part of your doctoral or postdoctoral project. This will, in turn, help you to understand how your university works and what support is available.

Certainly, we would expect postdoctoral researchers and those who wish to pursue a career within academia to demonstrate leadership in one of these areas, if not both. Establishing your own collaborative project is also a powerful addition to your CV, particularly if you are involving external or hard-to-reach groups. Event organising experience is always valuable whatever career path you take, because it uses many of the key skills discussed in Chapter 4.

One of the main benefits to you is that starting 'something' puts you in control: you are the one who decides on the initial aim and objectives and whom to invite to achieve these. You are the one who designs and invites the team you want to work with. You can invite others to join you and the team later; indeed, the people you invite will probably suggest other people to include. This is how networks grow. Furthermore, bringing together colleagues from different disciplines and organisations is inspiring and fun, and a key way in which, as researchers, we can advance our own knowledge and learning.

Before you can decide what kind of activities you might use to promote collaboration, there are several planning matters to be considered, which we consider next.

Planning an event or activity

As you begin to think about bringing people together to co-design, co-produce or collaborate on a project, some preparatory thinking needs to be undertaken. Specifically, you need to consider the 'who', 'what', 'when', 'where' and 'why' of any gathering. Addressing these questions will help to establish the purpose of the initial scoping event, what planning and funding may be required for it, as well as who must participate in it for it to be successful. All of this should be done *before* you decide on the specific format or type of activity you will use when you bring people together. Activity 9.1 will help you organise your thoughts. Always, though, take advantage of any training offered by your institution and make sure you ask advice of the experts!

Activity 9.1

Checklist to define the purpose of your event

In planning an event, you need to ask a series of fundamental questions, which will determine the kind of event you may need. Take a look at these questions and record your answers:

- What do *you* want to achieve?
- Have you identified the main purpose of the event? (If not, the next questions may help.)
- Do you want to experiment or explore ideas and possibilities?
- Do you want to use the activity for planning outputs or schedules of work?
- Is building new relationships the main reason for the event? If so, will this need to be a formal or informal event? Will you need to discuss how to work together at this event or at a later one?

The answers to these questions will help you to choose an appropriate activity. We will provide you with some examples of different kinds of activities in the next main section in the chapter.

There are other factors to consider:

- Will you need any resources?
- Are there likely to be costs involved?
- Will you be organising the event on your own or with others? If with others, who would you like to co-organise the event with and why do you want them?
- What would they contribute?
- What would their role be?

Learning to work with someone else to co-organise an event is in itself a collaboration. You will be collaborating to collaborate!

Once you have identified the purpose of an initial event, you will need to consider carefully who you want to engage with and invite to the event. Think about the number of people and whether they are internal to your university or external (or a mixture). This is important because, without the right people, you will not achieve your aims. In addition, the number and kind of people or potential project partners will play a major part in deciding what kind of event you want to hold. If you are uncertain about the best way to bring together the people you wish to invite to achieve your aims, we describe different types of events designed to help people collaborate in the next section.

In addition to the considerations mentioned above, there are some very practical questions that will help you to plan your event in more detail. For example, when do you want to hold your event? Are there any time pressures, such as a grant application deadline? How long do you want the event to last (which will depend on the type of event/activity you have chosen)? Do you need someone to facilitate the event or are you planning to do that yourself? Is it going to cost money? Before we deal with these very practical points, let us start with a best-case scenario in Reflection Point 9.1.

Reflection Point 9.1

Who would be in your fantasy collaboration team?

If money, people and connections were not an issue and you could create a collaborative project or engagement event of your dreams, what would it be and who would be in your fantasy team?

Why would they be on your list? (This question will reveal some fundamental characteristics about the people you should aim to include in a real event.)

To organise any kind of event requires time. Even a meeting involving a small number of people can take time to organise. A more ambitious event will have more elements, involve more people and take longer, even if you spread the load by devolving responsibilities to others. It is often best to start small, such as staying within your discipline or academic comfort zone by founding a group of like-minded researchers from your peers to co-design and co-author a paper, or to contribute to a blog. Irrespective of the size of the activity, it will still need to follow the basic project management rules. As you will know from planning your doctorate or your research project, time spent on planning at the beginning is time well spent. Events, no matter their size, may also require some money to be spent as well as time, which can be problematic.

Is there access to any money?

Depending on what you are planning to do, you are likely to need access to some money, if only for refreshments. The kinds of costs you are likely to need to cover are room hire, refreshments, publicity, a facilitator and expenses if you need to engage a key external speaker. Whatever the size of your event, access to some funds will generally make it easier, so it is worth exploring how you might gain access to financial support. Departments and Deans sometimes have funding to support small activities, and so a good starting point would be to ask your supervisor or line manager if they have any suggestions or are aware of any funding pots that you could apply for. Our sister book in the series, *Success in Research: Navigating Research Funding with Confidence* (Spencely et al., 2020), may provide other ideas about sources of finance.

If you are an early-career researcher (ECR) on a project, you might ask your PI whether there are any funds within the project you are employed on that could be used. You are more likely to receive assistance if your event links closely with the project or if you can demonstrate the benefit of your event to your project. It is always worth asking, especially if you can present a business case (as discussed in Chapter 10). Similarly, you can ask if your department or faculty has some research or general funds that could be used, particularly if the costs are low.

If you are a doctoral researcher funded by an external organisation, there may be funds available that you can use or apply for. These funds may be competitive or have specific deadlines, for example, if you are funded in the UK by a Doctoral Training Partnership, so you might wish to ask your contact at the funding agency in good time.

There may be university funds or competitions specifically to encourage collaboration or events designed for impact development, which your proposed event could be made to fit. Again, these are likely to be competitive and have specific deadlines. There may be annual deadlines for this type of funding, and it is important that you plan well ahead of time, checking the eligibility criteria to ensure that you can apply.

Talking to a mentor or involving senior colleagues can sometimes help to open doors to funding, although there is no guarantee of this. They might, though, be able to tell you where else to ask. We all know of doctoral and postdoctoral researchers who, through imagination, courage or sheer audaciousness, have obtained small amounts of funding from charities, local businesses, and publishers – of course they needed to offer the 'funder' something in return, albeit advertising opportunities, copies of the outcomes or reports. It may be that a commercial business or a professional group could have a vested interest in what you propose, for instance it may provide them with specific useful information, so consider what outputs or outcomes might eventuate and who would benefit from them beyond your working group. This kind of 'entrepreneurial' activity will be very useful, no matter what you do after this stage of your research career.

If there is no money available, it does not mean that you cannot run your event. The first thing to consider is whether you can revise your event plan to cut down on costs. If your venue costs money, investigate free alternatives. For example, if you book conferencing space at a university, there will generally be a cost involved. However, there are likely to be meeting rooms and teaching rooms available free of charge that can be booked through your department, school or faculty, or your Doctoral College/Graduate School or central timetabling. Talk to your Researcher Development department or Graduate School administration team who, if they cannot help you themselves, will be able to point you in the right direction. Refreshments also cost money, but your department or your Graduate School/Doctoral College might have a budget for this and can provide some basic refreshments for you. They may also have equipment, such as an urn or coffee machine, that you can borrow. If you are doing the catering yourself, then try to find a room near a kitchen because it makes life much easier if you can access hot water for drinks and washing-up facilities. Needing to provide lunch increases the cost of an event considerably, so another way to cut costs is to avoid lunchtime or, if it is an internal event, invite colleagues to bring their own lunch. Even if your university does not have a tradition of 'brown bag' lunches (a US term for a packed lunch), you can start a new trend.

If there is no funding available, paying expenses for external experts or speakers will be impossible. You might consider asking if they are able to fund themselves, although you will need to explain in advance that you cannot pay their expenses but would really value their input to this very worthwhile event. It would be embarrassing if they assumed you would pay for them and could not. Make sure that you clearly demonstrate to them why the event will be worthwhile, so that they can decide whether the cause is worth the lack of financial incentive. If you have a choice, find experts who live more locally as they are likely to be more amenable to funding themselves because travel expenses will be minimal.

Inviting people

Once you have sorted out the aims and outline of the event, as well as the practical and financial aspects, you will need to consider who to invite. This requires careful consideration. Assuming you have the time and funding (if needed), how do you identify the relevant stakeholders to attend your event? Are there key people that you must have there? Or would an open invitation be more effective? Once you have decided who you want to be there, how can you get their commitment to attending? One of the ways to do this is to make sure that there is an obvious benefit for others in attending – beyond what you will get out of it yourself.

Having the right people at an event aimed at facilitating collaboration will be key to the success of the event and in achieving your aims. Are there people whom it is essential to have attend? If so, it would be worth organising the date around the availability of those key people. See Top Tips 9.1 on the most appropriate ways of inviting people.

Top Tips 9.1

How best to invite people

1. Email is one way of inviting people to an event, but with the current culture of email overload, a calendar invitation might be a more effective way. If you are opening the event more widely, not just to targeted individuals, you may want to print posters, advertise on your intranet or get a slot in departmental meetings or newsletters to publicise it.
2. Make sure the invitation is concise but explains the aim and format (for example, a workshop or **sandpit**) of the event, as well as the start and finish time and venue. People are very busy so will only be persuaded to attend events if they can see an immediate or short-term benefit for themselves, and so it is important in your invitation to state the benefit or likely value to them of attending. You need to sell your idea: most professional people are notoriously over-committed, but they will go to great lengths to prioritise an event they really want to attend.
3. Always give a deadline for responses. Be realistic so that, if by that deadline you do not have enough attendees or you do not have confirmation from the key people you really need, you have time to reschedule. It is much better to do this than to go ahead with the initial date and fail to achieve your aims because of lack of participation. Remember that, realistically, it is very unlikely that everyone who wants to attend will be able to make the chosen date. If colleagues clearly are interested in taking part but cannot do so, keep a list of names and follow up with them, for example, by circulating the outputs of the event and/or inviting them to subsequent events.

If you are inviting people from outside the university to your event, there are additional considerations. You would generally offer them travel expenses and so on (as discussed above), but there is also the possibility of their asking for a fee to attend. This would be unusual, but it could arise, for example, if you invited an academic who has become a TV personality or who is, in effect, working as a consultant. This could significantly add to the cost of the event, so should be considered carefully, even if you have the funding to pay for them.

If you do engage externals guests, the perceived benefit to them would probably need to be greater or more fully explained than for internal invitees. Perhaps there are other people in your university or department they could benefit from engaging with, or they might be interested in visiting an on-site facility such as a specialist museum or archive. You could coordinate your event with another meeting or meetings, making it more worthwhile for them to attend, particularly if they have travelled from a distance. You may be surprised by the number of people we have met who simply are interested in visiting a university campus because it is outside their usual experience and are curious about what 'ivory towers' are actually like. They may also need directions to the venue and a booked parking space or information about trains, buses and taxis. Find out about this from your departmental administrator or Doctoral College/Graduate School administrator. These seemingly minor considerations are very important in helping to build the rapport we highlighted in Chapter 1.

Facilitating your event

As it is your event, you need to consider the role you wish to play in it. Do you want to lead the whole event or simply to introduce the session and talk about the aims and outline of the day? Alternatively, you might prefer someone else to do this. Facilitating events is not easy, so you could seek some support in the first instance. Further, you may favour someone independent to guide and lead the discussion. You could, for example, ask a senior colleague, researcher developer or member of Graduate School or research management office if they can help. It is particularly useful to invite people to help you who have experience of working collaboratively and perhaps have taken part in these kinds of events before. As with invited guests, you would need to explain the purpose of the event and prepare or 'brief' them in advance.

How to capture the key points

You will want a written or electronic record of your event; otherwise making the most of the outcomes of the event will be difficult. Audio-recording or filming is one way of doing this. There may be the appropriate technology available in your venue or you may need to bring someone in to provide it (check this when you book the venue). Even if the technology is in place, you might want to ask someone else to operate it for you. You will also need to ensure that all participants consent to the session being recorded, even if you are only going to use the recording privately.

If you are having break-out groups, you may need a few people who can lead the discussion groups. These could be attendees, but make sure you ask them in advance as this will save time during the event and will allow you to select people who encourage discussion rather than taking the opportunity to hold the floor alone.

It is good practice for someone to take notes in both full sessions and break-out groups. The easiest way to do this is to ask colleagues who are attending to take responsibility for the various sessions and to capture discussion output as it happens. As the event organiser, you will not be the best person to do this because there will be too many other calls on your time and attention.

One of the best ways of capturing group thinking is to ask everyone at the very beginning what they would like to achieve by the end of the session. To save yourself work recording it, provide everyone with a piece of paper and ask them to write down their goals. Collect all the suggestions and briefly review them for the benefit of the whole group. Being open and transparent or candid – that is, 'tell everyone everything' – is the key to collaborative success. Make it clear that you do not intend to discuss the points; rather, you wish to provide everyone with a view of the extent of ambition in the room. At the end of the session, return to the list of aims and check if they have been satisfactorily met. You will need to allow time for the group to digest this. The group may need to discuss any aims that have not been met, decide on their relevance and determine how they might be encompassed, if appropriate.

Revisiting goals in this way makes people feel they have been respected and listened to from the start. This will be a first step in embedding the group's decisions and thinking during the event and will help to build the team. There are other things that you can do to ensure that the event is successful, and we provide some prompts to stimulate your ideas in Information Box 9.1.

Information Box 9.1

Making your activity work on the day

Below is a set of questions that will help your event to run smoothly:

- How long before the event would it be useful to arrive at the venue to set everything up?

- Is the venue set up in a way that suits your activity?
- Does the technology work (if you are using any)?
- Do you have the post-its, paper, pens, flip charts you need?
- Have you thought about how to register attendance?
- Have you considered how to capture the key points?
- Is the catering ordered and laid out?
- Do you know what time and where catering will arrive?
- Will you be able to incorporate all the 'comfort' information in the introductory talk? For instance, do you know the location of toilets, if there is likely to be a fire alarm test, and what the arrangements are should there be an actual fire alarm?

What kind of activities can you run to promote collaboration?

In Chapter 8, we highlighted the importance of facilitating and promoting collaboration between group members by nurturing networks of trust. In this section, we focus on the kinds of activity that help to initiate collaboration and engagement. There are several different activities you can use to help people understand what you mean and intend by collaboration. We have listed a few of our favourites – all tried and tested – below. The focus and operation of each, however, are different, and the one(s) you choose will depend on where you are starting from and what you wish to achieve. While some of these activities are more complex to organise and run, a few can be used during the project to ensure collaborative relationships remain healthy. The majority, though, are useful when bringing people together to form a new group or project.

Before we present the activities, we should point out the importance of ensuring that all participants understand the terminology that is being used. For example, the term 'sandpit' is often used as a generic term to describe a variety of 'collaborative' activities. Clarify what you understand by it to those who are working with you. We have provided our definition in the Glossary.

Easy activities

Here are some activities that are straightforward and not generally difficult to run.

Idea storming

What is it?

Idea storming is a creative technique generally used to find suggestions to solve a specific problem. There are many ways to run these sessions, but all participants should take an active part and make suggestions. Participants should be encouraged to think as widely and wildly, and no idea is criticised. The intention is to be as creative as possible. Suggestions can be made verbally, written down on post-it notes or flip-chart paper, or electronically. Those suggestions are then discussed by the group as a whole and then further refined. Sometimes ideas that initially seem ridiculous are the germs of great ideas. In fact, this has been the basis of much innovative science and art. Whoever thought that putting a bit of self-sticking glue on small pieces of paper would turn into a massive stationery business and the mainstay of office and educational work?

When should you use it?

Idea storming works well as an initial activity, for example, to work out the breadth of a research challenge or to determine the skill-set needed for a project. It can be used as the first part of a longer collaboration session when you are encouraging all options into the open.

Positives and negatives

This is a good ice-breaking or kick-off activity, but the ideas then need to be used to ensure a productive follow-on. The facilitator needs to ensure that everyone contributes so that they feel part of, and take ownership of, whatever comes out of the activity.

Practical points: facilitating an idea storming session

Post-it notes are a staple of idea storming sessions. Physically getting participants to get up and put notes onto boards helps encourage engagement in the group. This can also be done online where there are numerous free tools advertised – including Google Documents!

A creative alternative to asking for solutions or positive outcomes is to engage in some reverse thinking focused on negative outcomes. This entails questions such as 'What would we need to do to make the worst X, or to make situation Y as bad as it possibly could be?' or 'What would the worst event in the world look like?', and so on. Since some people (risk assessors in particular) find it easier to discuss worst-case scenarios, this might be a fruitful opening activity, which you can later flip into a more positively worded exercise.

Dating and matching activities

What are they?

Dating and matching activities involve a series of short one-to-one meetings to discuss mutual interests with the aim of engaging participants. These are followed with more in-depth meetings with those participants who have something in common. Meetings can be organised either in advance by you as the organiser matching people with each other, or on the day by participants choosing whom to meet based on specific criteria or more randomly by using a speed-dating type of activity.

When should you use them?

Dating activities are a good way to provide the opportunity for those with common interests to get together, particularly to build up new academic collaborations. They can be very short and therefore can be used extremely flexibly, for example, for networking as part of a larger event or as a regular lunch-time session. They work best with a larger number of people, in excess of 15, so that there is a wider variety of opportunities for common ground or interests.

Positives and negatives

This method works well if you are trying to build up collaboration within the same institution. From our experience, if you want to encourage collaboration with non-academic partners using dating activities, it will work best if a more structured model is used. This will ensure external colleagues are meeting the right people and have a fixed appointment time.

Dating events can be short and therefore used as part of a longer event. The major disadvantage for you as the organiser is that it is very difficult to capture the outputs of these short meetings. You will need to rely on the participants themselves providing you with information, although you can provide writing materials to make this easier.

Practical points: facilitating a dating activity

For all dating activities you will need a venue with a large, flexible space that can be divided into meeting zones, preferably with some seating. Five minutes is not long to stand up for, if you are relatively healthy, but a series of five-minute discussions would require rather more comfort. It is also worth having some time after the session for people to network freely in case unexpected common interests emerge. Dating can also be organised on the day using sign-up sheets for allocated times and venues. As the organiser, you need to make sure that details of people's interests are available. For a more formal dating activity, you will need to collect details of participants' interests in advance and organise a 'programme', with allocated time slots and rooms (or tables), available to all.

The easiest activity to organise is speed dating but it still needs to be planned to avoid it becoming chaotic. We sometimes use coloured dots on badges or handout cards with images or animals on, and ask people with one colour, picture or animal to meet people with another, for example, blues meet with yellows or lemons with limes. Another fun way is to use rotating circles, rather like a party game, with everyone in an inner circle moving on after five minutes. A bell or whistle is very useful for calling everyone's attention when it is time to move on.

Ketso®

What is it?

This is an established commercial product with ethical and fair trade credentials that comes as kit in a bag. It was created by Dr Joanne Tippett, who developed it while conducting research in Lesotho (see Information Box 3.2). It has a specific pedagogy, whereby participants work in rounds writing thoughts on leaves in response to questions conceived by the facilitator in advance. The leaves are placed on mats and are discussed in small groups and eventually by the whole group.

When should you use it?

This is ideal in a wide range of situations where people need to share and develop ideas, such as during initial scoping through to planning. It is especially useful when people do not know each other, as the activity encourages group interaction, or when you need to work with external participants unused to working with academics. If you are new to facilitating, it is also a great tool for taking the pressure off the facilitator because you will be managing a process you have worked out in advance.

Positives and negatives

Ketso® is easy to use and very interactive. It is environmentally friendly, portable and reusable, and is excellent for bringing together different kinds of people and sharing ideas in an equitable way. Although the kit might be somewhat costly for individual researchers to purchase, it is worth asking around in case someone in your institution may have one you could borrow, or perhaps you could persuade the development and training unit to buy one. (Alternatively, if funds are very low, you could improvise on the method with paper and post-it notes, although the experience would be different.) To go through the whole process, from scoping to planning, will take time, usually a day, especially for a complex project. Alternatively, you could focus on one aspect of the process, which would take a few hours.

Practical points: facilitating a Ketso® event

You will need to pay close attention to the questions raised in the planning section above and draw up your questions in advance according to what you aim to achieve. Numbers will be limited to the number of mats you have. You will need about 30 minutes to set up the equipment, perhaps longer if the room needs to be put into **cabaret-style** or café-style (small groups around tables). You will need to allow planning time for the order of the questions.

Moderate difficulty

The following activities require more effort to arrange and operate.

Sandpits

What are they?

Sandpits can have a variety of formats but, from a research perspective, involve bringing together a group of people with knowledge in a specific area or a range of areas to discuss a research question or series of research questions. There will be clearly defined aims and objectives, which will have been communicated to participants in advance, together with the research questions. Some degree of resolution is expected by the end of the event.

When should you use them?

Sandpits work well when you need a very focused discussion around pre-defined topics. In the UK, funders often use them to bring multi-disciplinary groups together to address a specific research challenge. An example of this is the way that the Engineering and Physical Sciences Research Council has formalised the sandpit to suit their needs. This is explained on their website, the link for which can be found in the Further Reading section.

Positives and negatives

Sandpits work best when the objective can be well defined, for instance, to bring a group together to address a research funding call. They also work best with a limited number of participants (20–30). Because they are widely used by the UKRI to distribute pots of funding, attendees (at least in the UK) might expect some tangible benefit from attending. To achieve the specific outcome, you would need to ensure that it is well facilitated to keep attendees focused.

Practical points: facilitating a sandpit

To work well you need to allow at least half a day for a sandpit, but usually longer, which, from a practical point of view, increases the cost. You need to ensure you have ways (and people) to record the discussion and the outputs.

Focus groups

What are they?

These involve an organised discussion with a selected group of invited individuals with the aim of obtaining their views and experiences of a topic. The idea is generally to find out a range of views and experiences on the same topic.

When should you use them?

Focus groups tend to be used widely by market researchers and in qualitative social science research. They are a good way to interact with, and involve, members of the public, for example, when developing a research project.

Positives and negatives

Focus groups are not complicated to run; however, it is often difficult to identify the right participants for an effective focus group and excellent moderation is essential to getting the results you are looking for, especially if you wish to ensure that all viewpoints are elicited and recorded. They are valuable in encouraging the discussion of controversial topics or ones that people might be shy about declaring a viewpoint about on their own. Having others to argue with, or to support, your argument seems to evoke more information.

Practical points: facilitating a focus group

Focus groups tend to need a considerable amount of organisation, particularly when identifying and bringing in members of the public. Small groups tend to be more effective: 5–10 people are generally recommended. A moderator with good leadership skills is key to the success of this method.

Strategic/conversation cafés

What are they?

These, as the name implies, are discussions around tables in a café-style environment involving small groups of people. As with sandpits, the topics are determined in advance and placed on a table. Participants are assigned to tables or choose tables in advance and discuss that table's topic for perhaps 30 minutes before moving on to another table to discuss the next topic. Normally, each table has a facilitator who can capture the opinions of the participants and feed back to the whole group at the end of the session.

When should you use them?

Cafés work well when you need to capture a large number of views across a wide range of subjects in a short space of time.

Positives and negatives

To work well this activity needs several good facilitators who are able not only to capture the discussion efficiently, but also to organise the key points of the discussion and feed them back effectively to the entire group. This is another activity where to be productive, the participants need to be kept on topic, and so it does not work well without table facilitators.

Practical points: facilitating a café

The beauty of this method is that it can work with any number of people. However, the more tables you have, the more facilitators you will need. Each table also needs a flip chart or similar to record the discussion.

As the venue should look like a café, you can be very creative with the layout of the room. You could use paper tablecloths and ask participants to write on those. And you could produce discussion points or questions in the form of a menu.

More difficult activities

These activities are more challenging, and we advise researchers to enjoy participating in them rather than organising them in the first instance.

Inception meetings

What are they?

An inception meeting is an initiation meeting for a project. The meeting brings together all the participants, stakeholders and clients on a project with the aim of formally outlining the project aims, objectives, timelines, etc., and of confirming the roles that each group will play in the project so that everyone understands the common goals. This kind of meeting can last for several days. As a doctoral or early-career researcher, it is more likely that you will be involved in, or invited to, an inception meeting, rather than lead on one.

When should you use them?

Once a project is confirmed, the first meeting will be the inception meeting.

Positives and negatives

This is a better for large collaborative projects as they are time-consuming, expensive to arrange and require considerable organisation, especially if large numbers or very busy people need to be there.

Practical points: facilitating an inception meeting

In project management terms, the inception meeting is a formal meeting, and so will need a chair, agenda and minutes. Attention to the variety of speakers and participation formats will be required.

Open space events

What are they?

Open space technology (OST) was pioneered by Harrison Owen in the 1980s and events are unusual in that they start without an agenda or question; rather, the initial session identifies the topics for discussion, and anyone who suggests a topic must be prepared to lead a discussion group on it. The facilitator collects topics together and organises them into an agenda. Participants can choose which discussion group to join, and a key principle is that they can move to another group if they wish. Each discussion group lasts up to an hour, followed by feedback to the main group.

When should you use them?

This works well when people do not know each other, particularly if they are from different disciplines. One of the authors has used it effectively to elicit different research challenges, potential programmes and projects within a broadly identified area.

Positives and negatives

These events are quite challenging to run but have the advantage that the agenda that is set is 'owned' by the participants, who will be discussing issues that they have identified rather than issues that have been identified for them. Commitment is key to the success of this method.

Practical points: running an open space event

You need plenty of space for break-out groups and someone to take notes in each group. Flip charts and other aids for capturing points are essential.

Opposites attract

What is it?

This is a process for encouraging interdisciplinary activity (initially conceived by the University of Bristol). Individuals think about their research and come up with three terms that summarise the essence of their research. They write one word (or perhaps two or three at most) that describes their research on a post-it note or slip of paper. Participants discuss their three ideas in pairs and find ways of combining all six ideas into one project or outcome. This process can be scaled up once participants have warmed to the process. Participants then form small groups of 4–6 people, each person contributing at least one of their ideas to the group (if they use all three, it will be a bonus). Groups have a limited amount of time to come up with a collaborative project using all ideas generated. You can offer the groups a choice of making a proposal for such things as funding new research, a module for undergraduates, a video, an interactive display for school children or online course for the public.

When should you use it?

This activity works well when you wish to create multi-disciplinary collaborations. It is especially useful for creating new ideas and outputs that can form the basis of funding applications, new interactive tools with which to engage the public or for teaching students. It is also useful for introducing the ideas of co-production, co-design and interdisciplinarity to those unfamiliar with them. The outcomes will not be used but are a precursor to other events and activities. In this situation, it is essential that each group identifies and describes to the whole group the methods they used and how they approached the task. This will raise awareness of the process that can be built on with other activities.

Positives and negatives

Participants need to be flexible in their thinking and approach and the facilitator must be effective at encouraging the interchange of ideas. One advantage of this activity is that the costs are low and few resources are required. However, developing beyond the scoping phase may require funding, so you will need to be prepared for that.

Practical points: facilitating an 'opposites attract' event

The venue should be set out in cabaret style. Each person will need post-it notes or small pieces of paper to write their descriptor on, and you will need either flip-chart paper or an electronic means of recording the plenary ideas.

What to do after the event

In practical terms, how you follow up on your collaborative activity will depend upon what you and the participants were aiming to achieve, the nature of the activity itself and what subsequent actions (if any) were agreed. If you did not discuss how you will work together (team rules and conduct between members and so on) at your event, it is a good idea to plan to discuss this in the early stages of your collaborative endeavours. Immediately, though, you should reflect on the event, whether it achieved what you intended, and evaluate the participants' views. Key questions will focus on what went well, what did not go so well and what you would do differently next time. Irrespective of the outcome, be sure to celebrate the good points, and congratulate your team and everyone who contributed to make the event a success. Top Tips 9.2 makes some suggestions for your next moves if, at the end of the event, you find that you have not achieved your aims.

Top Tips 9.2

What if it did not go well?

1. If the activity did not result in meeting your aims or those of the attendees, then it did not go well. Soon after the event, gather your colleagues together for a 'wash-up meeting' (a debrief) to consider what went wrong and what could have been done to improve it.
2. If you asked attendees to complete feedback forms, use these to inform your meeting. Make sure you consider the positives as well as the negatives.
3. Use the experience to inform how you design and run your next collaborative activity.
4. Remember that the whole process is a learning experience for everyone and that even experienced colleagues face unsuccessful meetings sometimes.

There will always be challenges, but these can be minimised by good planning, preparation and a well-designed event. We leave you with our collaborative researchers' event checklist, and on a happy note, always keep in mind the last item.

Checklist 9.1

How to ensure a successful collaborative event

*   Establish your aims and objectives
*   Choose your activity
*   Find a date and time
*   Think about who you want to involve

(Continued)

- Put together a budget
- Find a venue
- Organise catering
- Invite attendees
- Get people to help on the day
- Find ways of recording what happens
- Pack a bag of practical essentials, including pens and post-its!
- Have a great time!

Further reading

EPSRC:Sandpits https://epsrc.ukri.org/funding/applicationprocess/routes/network/ideas/whatisasandpit/

Owen, H. (2008) *Open Space Technology: A User's Guide*. San Francsico, CA: Berrett-Koehler.

Pavelin, K., Pundir, S. and Cham, J.A. (2014) Ten simple rules for running interactive workshops. *PLoS Computational Biology*, 10(2): e1003485. doi:10.1371/journal.pcbi.1003485

Spencely, C., Acuña-Rivera, M. and Denicolo, P.M. (2020) *Success in Research: Navigating Research Funding with Confidence*. London: SAGE.

10

How can resistance be dealt with?

In this chapter you will consider:

- The internal and external challenges faced by researchers who want to collaborate and engage
- Strategies for maintaining feelings of control
- Strategies for building relationships
- Ways of convincing PIs and senior colleagues of the importance of collaboration

We hope you do not encounter resistance in your collaborative endeavours and while engaging with others. However, we, the authors, acknowledge that this can occur and believe that it is always useful to be prepared to counter any forms of opposition. This chapter explores some of the internal and external challenges that may be faced by you as collaborating researchers. We will consider strategies for maintaining feelings of control and for building relationships with partners, collaborators, supervisors and PIs. We invite you to consider also how to get supervisors and PIs 'on side' by convincing them of the importance of collaboration and engagement.

Challenges faced by researchers

This book is about encouraging collaboration, networking and engagement, which, although they are positive and rewarding activities, may not always be perceived as such. Resistance to them can take many forms – from the overt to the less obvious. The source can be external and even internal. For instance, on a personal level, collaborations can be a daunting prospect to the less experienced and less confident among us. In addition, researchers can feel that they are losing control, particularly when external partners, such as commercial or public partners, are involved as they may have their own agendas, drivers and priorities.

Resistance can also be intrinsic within the academy. Although academic networking is generally encouraged, not all PIs and supervisors see the benefit of their doctoral researchers and early-career researchers or postdocs (ECRs) taking time from their research to take part in public engagement activities, internships or other collaborative work not deemed as core to the specified research project. While we hope you do not encounter resistance in any form, we do believe that most, if not all, forms of challenge can be addressed and overcome. Consider Reflection Point 10.1, because often your personal stance can help to overcome any problems.

Reflection Point 10.1

E + R = O

E + R = O stands for Event + Response = Outcome. While you cannot change an 'event', you can control your 'response' to it. Taken together, they will affect the 'outcome'. This is an empowering little formula because you can always choose your response to an 'event'.

For example, imagine that your supervisor or line manager refuses your request to help with a public engagement event. Their refusal is an 'event' you cannot change – they said no. How will you react? What choices do you have? You could be angry and upset; you could accept the decision and not dwell on it; or you could ignore them and do it anyway.

There is usually a variety of ways of 'responding' to an 'event'. However, no matter which one you choose, there will always be a consequence or 'outcome'. In the above scenario, choosing to be angry and upset may damage your relationship with your supervisor or PI. Accepting their decision may cause you to change the way you approach your supervisor or PI with such requests in the future. Going ahead and doing it anyway is a risk – it may work out but it may damage your supervisor or PI's view of you.

The best course of action? We suggest try choosing to understand your supervisor or PI's position and see if you can negotiate a compromise.

There are several common challenges researchers may face when collaborating or engaging with others. We consider them in turn here before offering strategies in the next section of this chapter. First and foremost, there is the institutional level of contention.

Resistance at an institutional level

Institutional resistance is a useful way of describing something embedded into either the structure or the culture of the university which makes collaboration or engagement difficult to achieve. This kind of resistance can manifest in different ways and may be tangible or intangible. Tangible resistance, for example, might be a lack of support structures, such as funding, time or training. Intangible forms might be the attitudes or values within the culture of the organisation, exemplified by the prioritisation of agenda items, the number of people leaving a meeting before those items or facial expressions when topics are raised.

There is likely also to be much variation across the institution, so that some disciplines might be more attuned to working with the public, for instance, in the health and medical areas, while other departments or disciplines with less involvement and familiarity with the outside world may be less keen on external involvement. There may also be a clash of traditional and emergent (or new) ways of doing things. While many supervisors and PIs encourage joint proposals and conference papers between researchers within the academy, they may be less encouraging of time spent with industry or the public and charity sectors, for instance.

In Chapter 9 we discuss how to find support when you want to take the initiative and organise a collaborative activity. However, it may be that this kind of provision is not obviously available to you and your colleagues. You may find that within your institution there is a lack of support structures such as internal funding competitions to facilitate collaboration or initiatives such as networking events. It is always worth asking your Research and Enterprise office, or equivalent department, what they can provide with the aim of bringing people together. Activity 10.1 invites you to explore further the support within your institution. If you are in a single discipline institution, you may find that there is a lack of opportunity to collaborate within your workplace. You may also find that there may be a lack of training provision aimed at building the skills necessary to help you collaborate.

Cultural resistance may go hand-in-hand with structural challenges. If there is no structure or training to support collaboration and no opportunities to do so, then it may suggest that there is little priority placed on collaborative activity. As we indicated in Chapter 6, this is where national and/or institutional policy and strategy play an important role. Alternatively, there may be support structures and provision in place, but less importance placed on encouraging collaboration than on other activities. Historically, the academy did not place great value on public engagement work so, although this attitude has changed considerably in recent years, there is sometimes still felt to be a residual lack of genuine commitment to it. We are aware of some academics who have moved to other universities because their engagement work was not recognised or valued by their former colleagues. Fortunately, it is not the case that all institutions are unsupportive of such activity.

A question for anyone aiming to get involved in this kind of work is this: What kind of institution are you in and how supportive of collaboration and engagement is it? Even if the institution does not have a strategy for supporting researchers in these activities, there may be encouragement elsewhere. Is the department you are in, the colleagues and peers you work with, your supervisor or line manager supportive? See Activity 10.1 to review the support in your institution. The key point is to muster enough support, including people who can cheer you on, to sustain your activity. In turn, your enthusiasm may spread to others, creating a community of practice or new network.

Activity 10.1

What support does your institution provide?

Look at the list of support that might be available to doctoral researchers and research staff who are, or would like to be, involved in collaborative work. Identify which of the following your institution provides.

- Internal, interdisciplinary conferences or seminars
- Networking events
- Seed funding for collaborative projects
- Impact advice and funding
- Public engagement support and training
- Researcher development training
- Business development support

Do you know who or which departments to contact in your institution to enquire about the above activities? If not, think about how you can find out. You can ask your peers, supervisor or PI if they know of these activities in your institution. You can search the intranet and internet.

Resistance from senior colleagues

While leadership can occur in many different forms and at all levels – for instance, one can lead from the front, from behind or as a 'servant' – it should come initially from the top. Endorsement from senior colleagues is important in encouraging collaborative activity and behaviour at the institutional and departmental levels. The senior management of the university (or of the school or faculty) may have insufficient resources or be reluctant to spend the money necessary to put in place the structures that facilitate collaboration and engagement. They may be unable to provide the enabling funding, time or expertise that researchers may need.

This is probably not done with the intention of being deliberately obstructive, but resources are often short and there are many calls on time and money. There are likely to be many competing priorities to contend with. Senior management teams usually have targets to meet and may be concerned about allowing doctoral researchers to take time out from their studies for collaborative activity in case it affects their faculty or university completion rates (which may be used to measure university performance and hence government funding support).

PIs may object to early-career researchers taking precious time away from funded projects that are time-limited. Senior managers may also be concerned about giving doctoral researchers and more junior staff a public-facing role in case they say or do something that has an adverse effect on the public perception of the team or department or on the reputation of the university. This can be a particular problem for high-profile activities such as public engagement or engaging with important external partners. It can also be viewed as a potential problem in relation to ongoing collaborative endeavours; toes might feel trodden on. It also reminds us of some of the issues of building networks of trust that we discussed in Chapter 8.

As an early-career researcher, your PI or supervisors are your most immediate senior-level staff, and they may be resistant to you taking on collaborative activities. This resistance may take different forms. It may be 'active' resistance stemming from a reluctance to allow you to take time out from your core research. They may be concerned that this will adversely affect the quality of, or the timetable for, delivering that research. It is also useful to note that your supervisor's or PI's role and promotion prospects may depend very seriously on your completing the thesis or research project on time and within budget.

Appreciating the imperatives of others is an important professional skill to acquire and a quality integral to the Collaborative Code. They may be resistant because they themselves have never taken part in this kind of activity so have little understanding of it and no great knowledge of the wider benefits it can bring. It is also worth remembering that senior colleagues may themselves lack confidence in engaging externally or have been affected by an earlier negative experience. Therefore, one of your first tasks is to establish the source and the nature of the resistance, as this will be useful for choosing a strategy to overcome it. We will explore possible strategies in a moment, but first consider rating the institutional support you have access to in Activity 10.2.

Activity 10.2

Rating structural support

Consider the institutional checklist below and reflect on how well you would rate the level of support you receive for collaborative working.

Assess how supported you are by your institution, senior management, supervisor or PI and record this in the boxes. Is it high, medium or low?

	Institution (including professional service departments)	Senior management	Supervisor or PI
Internal, interdisciplinary conferences or seminars			
Networking events			
Seed funding for collaborative projects			
Impact advice and funding			
Public engagement support and training			
Researcher development training			
Business development support			

Will we refer to this again in Reflection Point 10.1.

Resistance from external partners

If you are seeking to collaborate externally, you may be supported by your university but find that the people or the organisation you want to work with are resistant to working with you. As with your own institution, there may be structural reasons for this resistance. The organisation may not be set up in a way that facilitates collaboration with a university or, particularly if it is small, may not have the capacity to adapt working practices to fit.

Similarly, there may be active resistance from individuals in an external partner organisation, for much the same reasons that you might experience resistance from senior colleagues in your own institution. Financial pressures are particularly likely to be a reason for resistance from senior management to collaborative activities in the corporate world and charitable sectors. Alternatively, it may simply be that they do not understand your proposed ideas.

The requirements, values and language or culture of business in public and charitable sectors can differ considerably from those of academia, as we noted in Chapter 3. Cultural resistance, in the general sense of ethos, can also be a problem for your potential external partners. This happens in all kinds of organisation but is likely to cause specific problems when you are trying to collaborate with hard-to-reach groups, for example, marginalised groups or particular ethnic minorities.

Susie Lund and Pam Denicolo's (2012) project to investigate Asian women's experiences of the provision of palliative care encountered some of these issues. Their article on collaborating with hard-to-reach groups is well worth reading for the insights it provides into how accepted research techniques, such as recording and transcribing, can be problematic in some cultural settings. Importantly, it also shows how overcoming these challenges adds to the research output (see Further Reading at the end of the chapter). See also Voice of Experience 10.1 on resistance between external parties.

Voice of Experience 10.1

Collaborating with the 'enemy'

I had a doctoral researcher who explored the collaboration between different social and health services. This was in relation to social issues such as teenage pregnancies and substance abuse. The researcher found that, most of the time, little came of these 'collaborations' because each participant group (including health professionals, social workers, youth workers and the police) were suspicious of each other. They saw it as collaborating with the 'enemy'! At the root of the problem, I think, was that the services were also in competition with each other in other respects as well as having different cultures and value systems, setting covert limits on the extent of the inter-organisational collaboration.

Doctoral supervisor – Psychology

Internal resistance

Not all the resistance you might face will come from others. Some of the most problematic forms of resistance to collaborative or engagement activity may come from within you. In Chapter 4 we celebrated the benefits of this activity, but we acknowledge that not everyone has the type of personality, level of self-confidence or skill-set that lend themselves easily to some kinds of activity. Those with quieter, more introverted personalities may find it more difficult to engage with others, particularly initially or in situations that make them feel vulnerable. Some public engagement activities, such as those involving presentations to a large or an unfamiliar audience, can be challenging; stage fright is common even in the professional theatre. While they may not appeal, or are best avoided, if you are new to collaboration and engagement activity, there are strategies that enable introverts to build their confidence, as we shall see below.

'**Imposter syndrome**' and self-sabotage are more serious forms of internal resistance and sadly not uncommon feelings among researchers, which may require specialist counselling or coaching to address (see also Ramsey and Brown (2018) for advice on 'feeling like a fraud'). However, the good news is that all these inhibiting characteristics can be overcome. Indeed, collaborating and engaging with others are some of the key methods for building confidence and for feeling positive about oneself and secure.

You may also be held back by a lack of knowledge. This may be in terms of identifying potential academic or external partners, or having a limited understanding of a specific situation or of the practical steps needed to take a collaboration or engagement activity forward (see our suggestions in Chapters 2, 3 and 5). Conversely, you may know what steps you want to take but lack the necessary skills to take them. For example, you may need training in presenting your work to a non-academic audience. These are all common concerns and none is insoluble. We provide strategies and practical advice to overcome them later in the chapter.

Even though you may have ideas, self-confidence, potential contacts or collaborators, and the necessary skills, you might still be holding yourself back from collaborating with others. Like your supervisor/PI, you may have concerns about how it could affect your work. It is natural to be worried about possible negative effects on your project; however, project management and monitoring skills can mitigate such problems, as we discussed in Chapter 4. Other common concerns may stem from not understanding how your work may be of interest outside your discipline or from being afraid that public engagement work may lead to the trivialisation of your research. Fortunately, experience shows that these are generally false assumptions. You will be surprised at who will be interested in your research, which is a morale booster. Far from trivialising your research, experience indicates that the opposite is usually the case, with researchers frequently improving their research as a result of being asked questions about it from completely different perspectives, as well as finding that the public views their work with great respect.

It is also quite normal to be concerned that collaboration might lead to you losing control over your research, taking it in a different direction from the one you had intended. While collaborative activity might make this happen, it is important to remember that research is a dynamic process. A change in direction could have happened in any case and can be very positive. Indeed, having a side project (sometimes called a second gig or hustle) is the way for postdoctoral researchers to begin to establish independence. It is a different issue if your concern is that, as a more junior researcher, others will colonise your ideas and make them their own. If you have these concerns, you must discuss them with your supervisor or PI immediately or seek advice from an ethical integrity office or officer. There are safeguards that can be put into place to prevent this, which we highlight below, but why not think about your positive attributes first (see Activity 10.3).

Activity 10.3

Positive contributions

It is easy to focus on the things we do not do well, or our weaknesses. However, successful people focus on their positive attributes and cultivate their strengths. Imagine you are invited to join the collaborative team of your dreams or participate in a prestigious public engagement activity. First, you need to present yourself for a friendly interview.

To prepare for the interview, list five key strengths or positive characteristics that you believe you have to offer to the collaboration or engagement. Remember these positive attributes and contribution when considering how to overcome resistance, which we discuss below.

Resistance during collaboration

Once you have initiated a collaboration or a collaborative activity, all parties should be keen to work together. Most relationships run smoothly, but there may be occasions when problems prevent the relationship developing as you had intended.

If you are collaborating with academic colleagues across disciplines, there may be language issues and conceptual understandings that hinder communication between disciplines. Every discipline has specific terminology and a different perspective on the same problem, and this difference needs to be overcome. One of the authors once facilitated an initial meeting to explore cross-disciplinary research collaboration in the area of mental health and found the group spent most of the meeting discussing and disagreeing upon what was meant by 'mental health'. Establishing and agreeing common understandings is one of the greatest challenges of interdisciplinary projects, and one of the most important to spend time addressing.

There may also be methodological issues that need to be overcome: methodologies that are well-recognised in one discipline may be viewed with suspicion by another. For instance, some scholars prefer methodologies that ask questions that produce qualitative data, while others prefer hypotheses solved by the production of quantitative results. Everyone will need to invest time in explaining and sharing areas and methods that are taken for granted in their own discipline, especially to those unfamiliar with or suspicious of them, to establish common ground. The issue of communication is exacerbated when collaborating with non-academic partners or in public engagement activities, where language use and understanding may be very different. Academic language as often opaque, full of jargon and difficult for non-academics to understand.

As well as different ways of communicating, collaborators may have differing objectives, as we noted in Chapter 3. A commercial partner may be motivated primarily by the need to improve productivity or profits when you are more interested in the potential of the research itself. This needs to be explored and clarified before the collaboration starts or there may be some serious problems ahead.

On a more pragmatic level, whenever you work with others, there is the possibility of personality clashes or differences in working style, which can be problematic. This is where adopting a professional stance by putting the aims and goals of the collaboration before your personal interests is important. You may also find that your collaborators have different levels of commitment to the project or there might be financial or logistical issues which were not anticipated at the outset. All these challenges must be confronted and overcome for the collaboration or engagement to be successful. The good news is that very little is insurmountable, as we shall see next.

Overcoming resistance

If you are experiencing any form of resistance, it is important to realise that it will often require persistence and patience to overcome it. Very often there may be no quick fix, and you may need to devise several strategies to resolve matters. The approach will differ according to the form of resistance encountered, and you need to bear in mind that you might have to deal with a number of these at the same time. Consider Reflection Point 10.2, which asks you to review how you rated the level of support in your institution in Activity 10.2.

Reflection Point 10.2

What can be done about rating support as low?

Reflecting on Activity 10.2, where you were asked to rate the level of support in key areas from your institution, senior management team, supervisor or PI, are there any areas that you rated as low? If so, why did you rate them as low? What would need to change for you to improve your rating? Do your peers and colleagues share this view with you? Is there anything you can do to raise the profile of the lack of support or provision? Can you lobby for action in the area to help improve the level of support and your satisfaction?

Dealing with all forms of resistance and finding strategies for managing and/or overcoming them all share a common starting point: you need to identify the real source of the resistance to be able to consider what is the best way forward.

Institutional resistance (academic and external)

If your institution or your external partner institution does not appear to have in place the structure and culture needed to encourage collaboration, as discussed at the beginning of the chapter, you will need to consider how to overcome institutional resistance. However, it is worth remembering that this may link closely to the attitudes of senior staff. By successfully dealing with one, you may be helping to overcome the other.

If you are taking the first steps towards collaboration, it will be very unusual if you do not need some form of support. If this support is not available in your institution, it is worth looking at other avenues. In the first instance, it is worth considering your professional or discipline association. Many of these provide events that will give you the opportunity to network or to engage with the public. Many also provide training courses that will help you acquire the skills you need. There are other organisations too, such as the UK National Coordinating Centre for Public Engagement (as discussed in Chapter 6), which provide training and opportunities. Look at the opportunities offered by research funders; some will only be for those working on projects that they have funded, but others may provide opportunities more widely. Any that are open calls will generally be competitive and often advertised alongside their funding calls.

Information Box 10.1

Examples of associations' and funders' support

Wellcome Engagement Fellowships: https://wellcome.ac.uk/funding/engagement-fellowships

North West Consortium Doctoral Training Partnership: Collaborative Skills Development Scheme, www.nwcdtp.ac.uk/current-students/funding-for-current-students/

White Rose University Consortium: Collaboration Fund, www.whiterose.ac.uk/collaboration-fund/

Social Sciences and Humanities Research Council of Canada: Partnership Development Grants, www.sshrc-crsh.gc.ca/funding-financement/programs-programmes/partnership_development_grants-subventions_partenariat_developpement-eng.aspx

Microbiology Society: Microbiology in Society Award, https://microbiologysociety.org/grants/events/microbiology-in-society-award.html

American Association for the Advancement of Science: Early Career Award for Public Engagement with Science, www.aaas.org/awards/early-career-public-engagement/about

---

You may find, even though public engagement or collaborative activity is not supported, that there are other activities within your institution which give you the opportunity to start along the path to engagement. Indeed, in our view, the role of researchers in academia and other sectors, as well as that of academic staff, is changing rapidly, so current generations of up-and-coming and early-career researchers should position themselves for future roles by making the most of the opportunities available now. There might be an outreach or widening participation department whose remit is to work with local schools, bringing pupils into the university and sending university staff to engage with them in schools. In the UK, universities are required by the government to do this kind of engagement activity. This can be an excellent place to start honing your collaborative and public engagement skills. If you happen to be in a discipline area where collaboration with schools is important for research, it may enable you to start building relationships.

Your marketing department or your alumni team will possibly run external-facing events for which they need speakers or academic colleagues to talk to visitors about their research. If there is no institutional culture of collaboration, they may find it difficult to engage more senior staff, which opens the door very nicely for those of you who are less senior.

There may also be organisations in your area run by doctoral students and early-career researchers which provide more informal opportunities to engage. A great example is the Bright Club in the UK, which has already been mentioned in Chapter 5. You can also organise your own events that interact with the public – the *café scientifique* model is a popular one (www.cafescientifique.org/index.php?option=com_content&view=article&id=72&Itemid=484).

There are other strategies you can put in place to overcome the different kinds of resistance that you may encounter. The key is to start small and to find positive, supportive (but not necessarily academic) colleagues to help you along the way. An example of 'starting small' may be to work with like-minded colleagues to organise an internal cross-departmental research discussion group. (Chapter 2 explains in more detail how to start small.) If you are encountering resistance that seems to be insurmountable, many of these smaller activities can be done 'under the radar' outside your department and in your own time. You can then start to gather the evidence and build the professional case you need to move up the scale.

Senior-level resistance (academic and external)

The first step to overcoming resistance from senior colleagues and from senior staff at an external partner organisation is to understand what is causing it (see our suggestion in Activity 10.1). The only way to know this is to enquire or to be curious about it. You can find out by asking directly or by exploring with other colleagues whether they have had a similar or the same experience. Once you have established the underlying reason, then you can start to address it. A head of department who has financial issues or performance targets is a rather different proposition from a PI who is concerned about the delivery of their research project. Both will require tact and sensitivity and the development of negotiation skills.

Having worked out what the problem is, you will need to put together a business case. This is to explain what it is you want to do, why and how you want to do it and the benefits to be gained from you doing it – that is, what is in it for them. You should also address potential risks and how you can resolve them, rather than ignoring them, hoping that they will not be thought of by your seniors (which is unlikely).

The first step in building your business case is to start to collect evidence for your case. The kind of evidence you need will depend on the reason for the resistance. For example, if the basis of the problem is financial, you will need evidence to show that you can run your collaborative activity with minimum or no financial input from the department. If the basis is concern about the delivery of the project, you will need evidence to show how it will not affect your ability to work effectively on the project, perhaps by means of a project plan to show how the two can co-exist without the research suffering adversely.

Once you have the evidence, you can use this to construct a 'business case' to support your cause. Information Box 10.2 details the process.

Information Box 10.2

How to construct a business case

The key points in constructing a business case are as follows:

1. Start with an 'Executive Summary', giving a brief overview of your paper before going into the detail.
2. Next comes 'The Opportunity': explain the situation and the opportunity that is being presented.
3. Then comes 'Analysis': explain the options available.
4. This is followed by 'Evaluation': assess the options, emphasising their value and benefit.
5. Finally, end with a 'Recommendation': describe your plan.

Always minimise jargon and be enthusiastic but clear and concise.

An effective business case is likely to be enough but, in some cases, if the resistance is deeply ingrained, you may need to do more to overcome it. You may need coaching skills to explore the resistance of the blocker (what is their real concern?), and then deploy negotiation and persuasion skills to make a professional and convincing case. It is important to understand the other's position and priorities in their terms, stand in their shoes, to reassure them and to help them move. It is important to use calm language and build trust, as we discussed in Chapter 8. Be open and invite others to choose the way forward; be compassionate and curious. Also, be prepared to have a back-up plan should your excellent skills not yield the result you want.

The last resort?

While we do not advocate 'going under the radar' as a first resort, if you genuinely can meet all that is expected of you and all of the deliverables on your Gantt chart, then what you do in your spare time is your affair. You must be mindful of meeting your existing commitments and, of course, of being alert to any health and safety, Intellectual Property, ethical and reputational considerations (as also discussed in Voice of Experience 10.2).

In the final resort, you may have to accept that the obstacles may not be surmountable until you are in a different position or organisation.

Voice of Experience 10.2

Going 'under the radar'

I began by taking on the lab tours in my research group for open days at the University. This was only an hour or two and I really enjoyed it. Then I received a general email asking for people to hold workshops in schools. I was excited about this, and my supervisors were initially supportive. I went into the lab early to get things sorted out, so was keeping up with my work. I really enjoyed the experience of explaining science to the school children. When the next opportunity arose to give a workshop again, I said yes. And then said yes and did it again and again.

Doing public engagement was beginning to fill a gap that I needed, personally. I had not felt very welcome in the research group, but through the public engagement activity, I was beginning to meet other like-minded people in the University. I was getting to know all kinds of people that I would not have met just by doing my research. I also was beginning to feel part of a community.

The feedback from the schools was great too. It made me feel valued because I was working in disadvantaged schools. Just going into the schools was a welcoming experience. I realise now that it was meeting a need that I was not getting from my research group. When my supervisors said that I could not do any more, I felt like I was being cut-off from a lifeline. That's when I went 'under the radar'.

I used my connections elsewhere in the University to help me with risk assessments, etc. But I also did everything my supervisors asked of me, and I did it to the best of my ability. I made sure there was nothing to alert them to my outreach work. When I set up a university-wide initiative, of which I am very proud, I do not think they were even aware it was my doing. My colleagues in the engagement community were, though.

Successful doctoral researcher – Engineering

Internal resistance

If you have recognised that you are resistant yourself to collaborative activity, yet you can see the benefits of it, then you have made the first step towards overcoming it. The next is to work out why you are resistant. If it is a matter of lack of knowledge or skills, this can be easily remedied by taking advantage of training opportunities at your institution or those run by professional bodies and by taking part in collaborative activities organised by others and to learn by observation. If you are not 'outgoing' yourself, there is no need to do this on your own; indeed, the whole point of collaborative working is to team up with people with different strengths. Try teaming up with a group of peers or choose a more extrovert colleague to work with. Also, it is important to remind yourself of your positive attributes and contributions and the five strengths you identified in Activity 10.3.

One of the main reasons for collaborating is to learn from others. If building your own collaboration or creating an engagement event is too advanced, then look for existing activities or opportunities, or training to undertake or get involved with. These will help to build your self-confidence. Chapter 2 provides some excellent ideas on starting small.

You can also find a mentor who can advise you and help you through the process. Many institutions run mentoring schemes with more experienced academics mentoring more junior colleagues, and a number also run schemes where researchers are teamed up with mentors from external organisations and businesses. See our sister book, *Success in Research: Mentoring to Empower Researchers* (Hopkins et al., 2020).

A mentor can also help you overcome your fears of losing control of your research or taking time away from your core project. Advice or training on how to plan your time effectively can also help you assuage these fears. If there is no formal mentoring scheme at your institution, maybe you can identify a role model and ask for their advice.

If you are concerned about others taking over your research or your research ideas, there are safeguards that can be put in place to protect your interests and your work. There are restrictions that can be used in relation to copyright and Intellectual Property. Your Library and/or Business Development teams will be able to advise you on these. When you are working on a research project with external partners, it is important that a legal agreement is put in place listing the rights and obligations of the working relationship. If the project is externally funded, then the funder will insist on this. Funders also have their own terms which the institution must sign up to before being awarded the funding (see another of our sister books, *Success in Research: Navigating Research Funding with Confidence*; Spencely et al., 2020). Your research office or legal team will advise you on this. It is important that you engage fully with them as they are there to protect your interests as a researcher as well as those of the institution.

We bring together a summary of points to help you overcome resistance in Top Tips 10.1.

Top Tips 10.1

Overcoming resistance

Here is a summary of things to consider when facing resistance:

1. Work out what kind of resistance you are facing.
2. Start small.
3. Be persistent.
4. Be creative.
5. Seek out supportive people – internal or external.
6. Take every opportunity to improve your skills.
7. Collect evidence of the benefits.

If you are serious about collaborating and can see the benefits to your research and to your career, seeking support of sympathetic senior colleagues to help you overcome personal issues is key. Ultimately, getting involved with an activity where you can articulate your own voice, receive feedback or assess people's reactions will be the best confidence boost there is. You will be astounded by how much you know and have to say.

Further reading

Hopkins, S., Brooks, S. and Yeung, A. (2020) *Success in Research: Mentoring to Empower Researchers*. London: SAGE.

Lund, S. and Denicolo, P.M. (2012) Collaborating with users: involving hard-to-reach groups in research – part two. *European Journal of Palliative Care*, 19: 136–140.

Ramsey, E. and Brown, D. (2018) Feeling like a fraud: helping students renegotiate their academic identities. *College & Undergraduate Libraries*, 25(1): 86–90, doi: 10.1080/10691316.2017.1364080

Spencely, C., Acuña-Rivera, M. and Denicolo, P.M. (2020) *Success in Research: Navigating Research Funding with Confidence*. London: SAGE.

Stover, S. and Holland, C. (2018) Student resistance to collaborative learning. *International Journal for the Scholarship of Teaching and Learning*, 12(2), Art. 8. Retrieved from: https://doi.org/10.20429/ijsotl.2018.120208

11

Following up and moving on: Concluding thoughts

In this chapter you are invited to consider:

- How to close or hand over a collaborative endeavour or project
- The unforeseen benefits of collaborations and engagements
- How to branch out on your own or with others
- The changing nature of collaboration and engagement work
- Some concluding thoughts

As we have seen in the previous chapters, some UK doctoral and postdoctoral researchers have been extremely active and enthusiastic supporters of collaborations and engagement for at least the past decade. Further, in Europe, the Erasmus programmes and European Research Area have encouraged researchers to become more mobile so that they can build partnerships and potential collaborations in the future. The changing policy and funding landscapes have not only changed research, encouraging more interdisciplinary projects and awareness of research impact, but have also transformed researchers.

In our final chapter we will point you towards the future in two ways: first, in terms of considering how you complete and move on with any collaboration and engagement. Second, we offer a few concluding thoughts based on our observations about, and experience of, the direction of collaboration and engagement for researchers.

Concluding a project or collaboration

Throughout this book we have focused on the benefits of collaborations and engagement. We have provided examples that range from taking initial steps within your university through to engaging with the public and then to building or being a member of larger collaborative partnerships. Like all good things, these will, at some point, come to an end. The considerations to be addressed then are whether it ended satisfactorily, whether people were clear that it had ended, and whether they had had an opportunity to reflect and provide feedback on the experience.

Having established a relationship and/or worked with a specific group or organisation, you now have the responsibility of ensuring that closure is managed appropriately. We all like a 'happy ending' and to part on amicable terms, if possible. Fortunately, people within and outside academia want similar things. They want clarity and certainty. They also want to be recognised and valued for their contribution and work, and to be thanked, preferably by the people in charge. They also want to share their stories with one another and/or tell a wider audience if possible.

For some researchers, this may mean handing over control to the supervisor, PI or other senior member of the institution, which you might be loath to do. However, it may be that management know-how is required at this point. It could also be that your research contract or doctoral research has come to an end, and a new set of researchers will build and develop that which you had a role in initiating. Alternatively, as a project expands, it might be that institutions may need to take a more proactive stance in supporting and advising researchers to protect and enrich their reputations. This should all be viewed positively.

While you may not realise the full outcome of your project or collaboration – for instance, where the work may eventually change policy – you can include it in any job application and on your CV. It will be valuable to note that you contributed to the initial work that led to a certain outcome, or that you gained experience from collaborating with 'x, y and z' in an impactful project. Everyone in the academic sector understands that it can take years, decades even, before the full impact or benefit of research is felt. It is less important that you were not the PI on a collaborative project or that you had successfully completed your doctorate before that major public engagement event took place. Rather, future employers, including academic ones, will want to know what your contribution was and how that has developed your skill-set. In addition, although you may not feature in papers written beyond your engagement with the project, you could write your own reflections on your experience with the work (bearing in mind any Intellectual Property issues, of course). You can, therefore, reap benefits from the experience long afterwards, including experience, learning, contacts, professional development and career stretch. Indeed, in ensuring that the handover to more senior colleagues goes smoothly and leads to the best outcome for all concerned, you will also be demonstrating the collaborative skills you have acquired.

There will be a variety of additional issues to consider at the end of a project or collaboration. For instance, it will be important to consider whether all your personal and group objectives have been met. If they have not, then how should this be taken forward? If it is your project or collaboration, then the decision may be yours, or it may be that this is the point at which you need to work with more senior colleagues to advance the project. If you and your partners wish to continue working together, then there might be financial and practical issues to consider as a group. A cost/benefit analysis of maintaining the collaboration should be undertaken with serious consideration given to how to obtain the necessary resources. No matter how much you have enjoyed working together, it is important to make the decision objectively and in a timely manner, so that if the decision is that the best course is to bring the collaboration to an end completely, you can manage your exit and project closure in a positive way.

Even if this was a small, initial collaboration, such as setting up a discussion seminar with a fellow researcher, you would always want to end it well. The contacts made during even a small collaboration are key to building your networks and to future collaborations, and many will become close friends and colleagues. A major part of ending well is to keep your original promises and fulfil your obligations. If you agreed that you would share a report or publication with a partner, then, of course, you should do so. At the same time, if you organised the project or collaborative activity, make sure you thank everyone for their contribution, either in person or by email or more formally with 'thank you' cards. Choose whatever seems most appropriate to the group culture.

Celebrating is also very important at the closure of the project or initiative and should be built into your project planning. Although this is particularly important for larger projects, no matter how small your activity, you should proudly promote it to as wide and as relevant an audience as possible. First, ensure that all permissions, such as those needed for copyright material, have been obtained. Companies, universities and other organisations may have press offices that will need to be consulted and whose approval you may need first.

You can celebrate by using the project blog page or website, Twitter or other social media, or you may want to go further by involving the press and the conventional media. If you do want to promote to the media or press, your university press office can also help you with this. However, celebrating is more than promotion to the outside world. An informal event for partners is a great way to round off a collaboration and to thank all concerned. We have some suggestions for other closing activities in Information Box 11.1.

Information Box 11.1

Some examples of closing activities and events

Here are some examples of closing activities and events you could use:

- Wash-up meeting – to discuss what happened and to resolve any outstanding issues.
- Impact assessment – to focus on the effects, benefits and achievements of the activity.
- Evaluation reports – to review wider aspects of the project, from design to impact.
- After Action Reviews – a specific post-project method to explore what should have happened, what did happen and why they differed.
- Exit interviews – to allow people to speak freely about their experience, often to a neutral person.
- 'Thank you' cards – to act as a souvenir as well as to note contributions.
- Social event – to celebrate a job well done.

Reviewing the whole process of collaborating and engaging may be a requirement of funding and the project itself, and thus something that must be done. However, if this was an independent or smaller collaboration, then you should plan to do this in any case. If the collaboration was something you led yourself (such as organising a seminar) or did 'under the radar' (such as a public engagement activity), then a review is particularly important.

Evaluations and unforeseen benefits

Collaborating and engaging with others can bring a host of unforeseen benefits, not only while you are working together, but also subsequently when the collaboration or engagement ends. Therefore, it is important to be able to evaluate the process as well as the product or outcome while tying the activities and connections together at the end. This will ensure you obtain the most benefit from the experience.

Key to any evaluation and assessment is honesty and openness. Self-assessing, being self-aware and appreciative of what has improved, and recognising what was valuable about the collaboration or engagement are essential. You should assess the quality and level of the contribution you made alongside that of your collaborators. This might be difficult; however, it is important to remember that this is not about whom you like or got on well with, it is about the work. It will require you to take a step back, setting personal feelings aside, and to consider why people remained involved and what they contributed. You should also evaluate how fair you have been in your assessment of others.

Better yet, invite them to share what they thought was valuable about the project and their contributions. You may obtain viewpoints and insights you would not have considered important or were simply unaware of. These may surprise you, but they will remind you that everyone sees and experiences things differently. What you have enjoyed most may contrast with what your other collaborators enjoyed. Consider Reflection Point 11.1.

Reflection Point 11.1

What was in it for them?

Think about the people you have collaborated, engaged or worked with most closely recently and what you have done together. Then reflect on how you think they might answer the following questions:

- What did you enjoy the most from working on 'X'?
- What did you enjoy the most from working together/with me?
- What would you have done differently or change if we worked together on 'X' again?
- How might their answers to these questions differ from yours?

If you do not know what your collaborating or engaging partners would say, be sure to ask them next time.

Ideally, if you want to have a closing interview, you will have discussed this at the initial planning stages so that everyone is aware and agrees that is what is expected. A simple question like 'how was that from your perspective?' indicates and confirms your collaborative stance and is a straighforward question that can open a rich seam of feedback. While it indicates that you are interested in hearing the others' view, it does mean you must listen to the answer and appreciate what people have to say – even if it is critical. This will be good feedback for you to reflect on later. Applying the respectful and inclusive approach throughout the project and right to the very end, as we identified in Chapter 1, will also secure your reputation as a collaborative researcher. Your reputation may have unforeseen benefits in that one of the people you encountered and made a good impression on may recommend you for another project or to one of their contacts.

Even if you were not the PI or leader of the project, there is much to be gained from sending an email or card to the people you engaged closely with or worked with, letting them know how much you enjoyed working with them. Even if, in truth, you did not enjoy working with them, there is no need to be churlish; you can focus on the benefits of the project and thank them for being involved.

The world of research is relatively small; yesterday's collaborator is likely to appear again in another guise later in your career, so it is wise to be generous when you can be. After all, there is always something to be learned from both good and less enjoyable encounters, even if only not to do it that way again – which is another unforeseen benefit. Your colleague might well feel that way too.

It is important to remember that all the people we engage with may need our help in future and hopefully will reciprocate by providing us with support when necessary. Perhaps it is a contact in a specific sector or subject, a potential co-investigator or partner in another funding application, an external examiner or simply someone to speak to your class of students about what they do. This is the exciting aspect of collaborating and engaging with others; by making new contacts, who may become our new friends, we simultaneously extend our networks and range of expertise.

Voice of Experience 11.1

Our experience!

We, your authors, although individually experienced in 'collaboration and engagement', had not previously collaborated with each other. Some of us did not know each other either and had to be introduced. We had all, however, worked with the colleagues involved as authors and editors for this book series in several very different ways over several years. The result of this is a new collaboration which is leading to exciting opportunities to work together in the future.

Branching out on your own?

Having gained new insights and skills, you might want to use the experience and connections to forge your own successful futures either by 'going it alone', in the form of freelancing or consultancy, for instance, or by setting up a small business or company. Many academics take on consultancy in addition to their main roles, and it is common for many people to have a side-project, as we have alluded to previously. If your choice is to set up your own business or consultancy or to go freelance, you will need to take advice on a range of related aspects.

The most important issues will be tax liabilities, and Intellectual and Commercial Property. The authors have all provided advice to other institutions or colleagues as freelancers. In our experience, declaring and paying additional tax in the UK is straightforward (the tax office is always willing to take more money), but you should check how that is done in your own context. If you are using ideas created while at a university, the Intellectual Property and Commercial Property Rights will all need to be considered by a professional legal advisor. The Intellectual Property Rights of institutions tend to be complex, especially if you generated ideas while in paid employment with them, so again, take professional advice about what you can or cannot use when you become independent. You should also investigate insurance issues because it is probable that any insurance that covered your activities while you were an employee or doctoral researcher will stop if you establish your further work as independent from the institution. It may be that membership of your professional body provides some protection, but this is also probably limited to specific activities.

If you are intending to do consultancy work while employed as an academic at a university, you will also need to ensure that you speak to whomsoever in that institution deals with Intellectual Property and consultancy for advice. These are precisely the issues that they are there to deal with.

We raise these topics here to alert you to areas you will need to consider and take advice on before branching out on your own. However, certainly do not think of these as onerous issues that will preclude you adventuring further. Indeed, some institutions are very supportive of researchers engaging in this kind of work and may be able not only to provide advice, but to help you to 'incubate' your ideas and provide insights into investment opportunities (see Chapter 3). They may want a fee or take a percentage of profit; however, there are lots of different arrangements and possibilities for you to consider in terms of what is best for you and your idea.

All the traits and skills acquired through collaborating will be invaluable, but a special one is the skill of knowing when to draw on the expertise of others and when to ask for help. Another is being prepared for a future shock, which is prevalent in this age of rapid change. This involves being both flexible in drawing on your acquired skills and prepared to continue learning other skills.

The changing nature of collaborating throughout your career/life

It would be very difficult, in our view, to avoid collaborative working and engaging with others in one's career. The steps you may have taken as a doctoral or postdoctoral researcher should provide a solid foundation for the future. You can ensure that the elements you have valued most from collaborating and engaging with others can be maintained throughout your career in different kinds of roles; however, the nature of these relationships will change over time, as illustrated by Pam Denicolo's Voice of Experience 11.2.

Pam's trajectory demonstrates the expanding nature of her academic collaborations in an academic career spanning some 40 years. This is, of course, only one example. While we would anticipate that your future career experience may include a range of sectors, users and partners, as does Pam's, the nature of those collaborations as well as your individual choices and opportunities, will influence the route your career takes.

Voice of Experience 11.2

An academic lifetime of weaving disciplines and roles

How collaborative working and engaging with others changes over the course of a career

In common with most academics, the predominant theme of my life is simply the weaving of roles related to family (too complex for this book) and work, including teaching, research, writing, administration, management, and executive roles in organisations and associations. My theme feels singular, at least unusual, in that it crosses disciplinary boundaries in teaching and publishing, and in the supervision and examining of many doctorates. That variety is what has made it interesting and maintained my passion, even though sometimes it has been wearying and often challenging. Indeed, I have only survived the rigours of being a career academic because of the support and stimulation provided by my many co-conspirators. I began as a relatively independent researcher/scholar, then projects and publications increasingly involved collaboration with doctoral researchers, academic colleagues or professionals in the health and social care sector; the most recent ones heavily involve collaboration with completed doctoral researchers, Researcher Development colleagues and others passionate about developing the doctorate and postdoctoral research. Without them, there would be less fun and a lot of boredom.

See the summary in Table 11.1.

Table 11.1 Academic collaboration over a writing career

Decade/roles (academic focus)	Journal articles	Chapters and books	Research projects and reports	Policy documents	Editorships	Course materials and DL modules
1980s – Postgraduate Researcher and Lecturer (Science/ psychology/teacher education)	4/2	2/1	2/0	0	0/1	6/5

(Continued)

Table 11.1 (Continued)

Decade/roles (academic focus)	Journal articles	Chapters and books	Research projects and reports	Policy documents	Editorships	Course materials and DL modules
1990s – Reader/ Course Leader/ Research Director	7/5 (2)	4/6 (5)	3/2	0/3	0/3 (3)	1/3
(Pharmacy/ psychology/ professional development)						
2000s z– Professor, Director of two Multi-disciplinary Centres	4/7 (4)	4/4 (3)	3/3	0/4 (1)	0/3 (3)	1/3
(Pharmacy/ psychology/ professional and doctoral development)						
2010 to date – Emeritus/ Consultant	2/8 (5)	5/14 (5)	1/2 (2)	0/4 (1)	0/2 (1)	0
(Psychology/ professional and doctoral development)						

Legend: Number of Sole activities/Number of Collaborative activities

(Number of international collaborations)

Does not include doctoral theses supervised but does include writing collaborations with previous doctoral researchers.

Concluding thoughts

Throughout this book we have aimed to demystify collaboration and engagement, providing practical advice and guidance as well as demonstrating their benefits to doctoral and early-career researchers and to those who support them. In today's research environment, proficiency in working collaboratively and confidently with others, and engaging with global challenges and external partners have become part of a fundamental skills-set for all researchers.

We have, hopefully, given you some tools to enable you to address research challenges through cross-disciplinary collaborations and engagement with the public, policy makers, corporate and non-governmental organisations. We expect researchers in the near future to be comfortable with collaborating across a wide variety of boundaries, whether they are disciplinary, organisational or sectoral. See Activity 11.1 and consider what you would like to do in the future and with whom.

Activity 11.1

What would you like to do?

If you could do anything you wanted, what would you like to do and with whom? Consider the table below and whether you would prefer to collaborate or engage with people in the main areas of activity. Tick those that appeal.

I would like to collaborate	I would like to engage	with....
		Academics
		The public/publics
		Industry/commerce
		Charities/NGOs
		Other professional groups

Looking towards the future, we anticipate the greater involvement of end-users and public engagement in research, including in the co-creation, co-design and co-production of research. This is a very different world from the image of the lone scholar in their, perceived, ivory tower. Indeed, reaching out to the public and organisations beyond the academy reminds us of the open discussions conducted in the olive grove dedicated to Athena with which we opened this book. We, the authors, with our practitioner hats on, would advocate researchers 'get out more' to meet with and discuss with others in this respect. We are passionate about the benefits of collaboration and engagement. We have aimed both to inspire you and give you confidence to take the initiative in collaborating with others.

In compiling the different elements of the book, it became clear to us that there are several key messages that permeate it. First, it is important to use your initiative and grasp the opportunities as they arise. However, it is much easier to progress on your collaborative journey with structural (and practical) support from your institution and from senior colleagues, such as supervisors or line managers or your PI. Universities appear to be moving in this direction, providing more of the support that researchers need. However, they could do more to recognise and appreciate the value of this work. We are hopeful that this will emerge. Policy initiatives locally (even at departmental level) and at a national or regional level, go a long way in nurturing activity in this area. Funding also helps considerably in facilitating collaboration. These were the lessons drawn from public engagement, Doctoral Training Partnerships and Knowledge Exchange Partnerships in Chapters 6 and 7. While creativity, imagination and persistence can solve many problems, policy initiatives and funding are needed to make the general direction of travel sustainable.

It has become clear that there is a wide and expanding range of opportunities in universities, which we have demonstrated and illustrated with examples throughout the book (particularly in Chapters 2 and 3). To make the most of them, it is vital that doctoral and early-career researchers take advantage of the training that is on offer, as well as leveraging the internal and professional expertise and best practice that is available to them. Sometimes feedback from those researchers bemoans the lack of a 'research community'; it seems that they have not realised that they are that research community, so they must be proactive in engaging with each other and other researchers, near and more widespread.

There has been the rise of a new cadre of professional in higher education over the past two decades, often described as **'third space professionals'**, a phrase coined by Whitchurch (2008). They are the researcher developers, research managers, impact managers, collaboration managers and public engagement professionals found in a growing number of institutions. These people are not traditional service professionals such as finance officers might be; rather, they form the bridge between traditional and non-traditional academic activity, often brokering between researchers and new forms of university activity. Many of these third space professionals have considerable academic experience as well as their own specialist knowledge and expertise. This is an emergent form of institutional resource, often not as visible to supervisors and PIs as it could be, yet one to which researchers need to be alert. When we asked you in Activities 2.1 and 10.1 to list the support your institution provides, we hope you included some of those third space professionals on your lists.

Most importantly, researchers need to have the confidence to learn from their own experiences. We recognise that is not often easily achieved, particularly as doctoral and postdoctoral research careers can be precarious and short. This makes it even more important that you make the most of the abundant range of opportunity proffered by your institutions and your own research. When they take such opportunities, researchers find they have something to say, and are generally astounded that others are greatly interested in this too. Collaborative work and engaging with others have tremendous benefits for researchers, not only for developing the skills you need, but also for your confidence development and well-being. There are benefits too for those who supervise and/or line manage researchers, and for their institutions, as we sought to show in Chapter 4.

Clearly, the researcher role is changing. Not only do we expect following generations to increasingly collaborate and engage with others, to build more innovative research and tackle challenging research topics, but we also anticipate the projects to increase in scale as they become more international, more complex, more diverse. This matters even if you leave the academy because you will then become the other partner in the collaboration: the person in the professions, business or industry with whom researchers will engage.

Fortune, as Louis Pasteur said, favours the prepared mind. We hope our little book has provided you with some ideas to help and inspire you on that journey.

We leave you with a final Information Box 11.2.

Information Box 11.2

A REMINDER: The 7Cs of collaboration

We think it is worth reflecting again on the 7Cs of behaviour that make up a Code of Conduct for collaborating and engaging with others:

1. **Compassionate** – everyone must respect others' perspectives and points of view, and welcome the disruption that other perspectives bring.
2. **Committed** – everyone must be committed to the working relationship.
3. **Curious** – everyone must be curious about other ways of thinking and doing, and why things work, or do not work, as planned or intended.
4. **Candid** – everyone should be honest and open with each other about how work is progressing and impacting.
5. **Creative** – everyone should embrace novelty, be adventurous, and play around with ideas.
6. **Constructivist** – everyone should be prepared to meet the unexpected as collaboration and engagement are active processes developed through all parties involved, making the sum greater than the individual parts.
7. **(un)Certain** – everyone should be able to manage uncertainty – who knows what the results will be! However, that is the fun of undertaking research and this kind of work in the first instance.

Further reading

Whitchurch, C. (2008) Shifting identities and blurring boundaries: the emergence of Third Space professionals in UK higher education. *Higher Education Quarterly*, 62(4): 377–396.

APPENDIX A

Being collaboration ready

Consider the questions below and select the most appropriate response.

Question	Your answer	How to prove and improve
Can you communicate your research clearly to others?	Yes	You are a great communicator and regularly talk about your research to others in a clear, effective way. You should continue to test this by asking people in your department to describe your research and asking your supervisor or PI to give you feedback.
		Getting an international peer network together to practise with is a good way to make sure your explanations are clear across language differences.
	No	Practise summarising your research in writing and getting feedback from your supervisor, PI or friends. Once you are comfortable about your written explanation, try using that as a script for when you talk about your research to people. Use peers in your department to practise on, or a critical friend to help you practise. Give them your summary, then one or two days later, ask them to give you a verbal summary of your research. Can they? Is it the message you want others to remember when you tell them about your research? If not, keep practising!
	I do not know	Give an informal talk about your research in your department. Ask someone other than your supervisor or PI to summarise your research. Can they? Is it the message you want others remembering when you tell them about your research? If not, see above.
Are you visible in your field, and is your willingness to collaborate clear?	Yes	Your university webpage and any internal pages are up to date. You have given seminar talks in your department or given a guest lecture. Your peers and your supervisor or PI know you are open to collaboration. You have a clear understanding of what types of collaboration your supervisor or PI will give you their support for.

Question	Your answer	How to prove and improve
	No	You need to make sure the right people know you are interested in collaboration and have a way to approach you. (Is your email visible on a University directory? Are you on ResearchGate and LinkedIn?).
		At a minimum, your supervisor or PI should know your willingness to collaborate, and you should ask them to introduce you or recommend you to others. Being searchable on the web is vital; make sure key words in your field are in your descriptors on social media, professional accounts and on group webpages.
	I do not know	Does your name and contact information come up in a quick web search of your field? Is it paired with your name or University? If not, see above.
		If so, make sure all the information is up to date, and think about ways you can increase your profile either through conferences or sharing links to your publications with your contact details.
Do you know what relevant others are doing and are interested in?	Yes	Collaboration is not just about putting yourself out there and casting a net; you must go fishing too! You make a habit of talking to other researchers about their work and show genuine interest by taking note of their key points and interest areas. You regularly attend University seminars and conferences. You follow and engage with other researchers' social media or professional accounts.
	No	Start attending more networking events, and make it a goal to learn about at least one other person's area of research. Start small and grow from there. Make sure you are using your professional and social media accounts as two-way communication tools. You will be surprised how much a retweet or a 'like' may stand out to someone else.
	I do not know	Can you clearly summarise some of your immediate peers' research? What about some of the leaders at your University? Are you aware of the trends in your own field or relevant topics being discussed? If not, see above.
Do you know how to prioritise your time and manage what you do?	Yes	You have an up-to-date calendar with standing meetings, major research milestones (such as conference abstracts, grant proposals, etc.) indicated, and an adequate method for time-keeping to keep track of your weekly capacity.
	No	Start by looking at your daily schedule. By keeping an Activity Log (see MindTools online for an example) for a few days, you can build up an accurate picture of what you do during the day, and how you invest your time. This will help identify time stealers and where you might be able to free up time for something else. Next, to collaborate you will need to set up meetings and schedules with your collaborators. To do this, you need to have an accurate calendar. For internal collaborations it may be useful to use whatever platform your University uses for this, so others can see your availability. Start by populating your standing events such as regular meetings, seminars, and any teaching or classes you may be doing. Then begin to fill in the bigger picture with conference dates, output goals such as paper submissions.

(Continued)

Question	Your answer	How to prove and improve
	I do not know	If someone asked you if you could collaborate on a project and they would need a preliminary project summary written up by the end of the week, would you be able to give a strategic 'yes' or 'no' to that request? Would you be saying 'yes' without knowing if you have time? Could you offer a compromise, such as 'I can't have an entire summary done, but I can give you some bullet points by tomorrow to work from'? If you could not offer an informed reply, you may want to look at the advice above.
Could you quickly respond to a collaboration request with the relevant material (such as an up-to-date CV, biography, publication list, written summary of research, areas of interest, or business card)?	Yes	You keep an up-to-date CV that is tailored to various purposes (including a two-page brief for grant proposals, a skills-based CV for team building, etc). You have an easily accessible list or folder of your publications you can share, as well as some sort of stock statement you can tailor which highlights your areas of interest and background. You have an up-to-date biography ready for seminar advertisements.
	No	Perhaps the most crucial of the items listed above is the CV. Having an up-to-date CV from which you quickly pull your publication list, personal statement, skills or job experience is essential, enabling you to respond quickly to those: 'I have you in mind for a project, could you send me a brief outline of your experience in XXX?' requests. Typically, if you are giving a seminar within or outside of your institution, the organisers will want a brief biography either for an introduction or to email out with an invitation. Be sure to have one ready and up to date. Having a readily accessible, organised folder where these documents live will maximise efficiency in these replies, so you do not need to spend a whole day crafting them.
	I do not know	Do you know the format requirements and do you have up-to-date CV versions for the funding agencies relevant in your field? If someone asked for a bio-sketch to accompany your seminar talk, would you have that ready to go? If a potential collaborator wanted your papers to read through, would you have those easily accessible either through an online platform or soft copy? If not, see above.

APPENDIX B

Spot the skills solution

Here is the list of all the attributes (skills, behaviours and qualities) that were discussed in Chapter 4 that collaborating and engaging enable.

1. Able to reflect on, or review, the range of your (management) skills
2. Effective time management
3. Effective project management
4. Effective financial management
5. Effective people management
6. Able to adapt management tools
7. Able to adapt to people (situational leadership)
8. Able to adopt a flexible approach
9. Able to plan a schedule of work
10. Able to monitor project progress
11. Able to allocate tasks fairly
12. Able to realign tasks when required
13. Able to identify who will lead the project and how
14. Able to identify who will keep the project on track and how
15. Able to identify who and how everyone will be kept informed
16. Able to evaluate progress
17. Able to respond proactively
18. Enquiring attitude
19. Transparent in dealings
20. Accountable
21. Able to hold 'difficult conversations'
22. Able to spot a 'false consensus'
23. Able to understand (or be able to identify – ask about) people's needs, their aims and agendas
24. Able to make decisions – especially critical ones
25. Able to make timely decisions
26. Able to convey difficult decisions

27. All-round awareness of what is happening or not working so well
28. Able to use and build on experience (to recognise the signs of difficulty in the future)
29. Able to adapt and respond to the situation
30. Able to adopt a continuous improvement approach
31. Able to listen
32. Able to acknowledge other people's viewpoints
33. Able to give feedback
34. Able to receive feedback from others – in good spirit
35. Alert to different styles and personality types – yours and others
36. Able to develop appropriate strategies (to facilitate personal interaction)
37. Able to be strategic
38. Know when to compromise – be political
39. Able to negotiate
40. Able to construct and present a business case
41. Able to record benefits for impact
42. Able to compile funding applications
43. Able to identify and present potential impact to funders (write proposals)
44. Able to report on impact for funder(s)
45. Able to write evaluative reports
46. Know when and from whom to ask for help and advice
47. Know your team members and their styles for managing work
48. Cognisant of your own working preferences
49. Able to evaluate (understand and recognise the impact that different working styles have on others and the performance of the team overall)
50. Able to consider the advantages and disadvantages, benefits or otherwise, of an activity
51. Able to assess team performance
52. Able to assess individual performance
53. Able to identify strengths and those of the people around you
54. Able to conduct risk assessment and manage risks
55. Able to assess ethical implications and seek approval where necessary
56. Able to assess the quality of work outcomes
57. Able to adapt work to a diverse range of people and in a diverse range of settings
58. Capable of adopting and adapting to inclusive, interdisciplinary and mindful ways of working
59. Able to celebrate your skill-set and attributes and those of others
60. Self-aware (alert to those aspects you may need to develop further)
61. Appreciative stance
62. Non-judgemental conduct
63. Accessible to others
64. Understanding of others
65. Able to persuade others
66. Able to manage resistance
67. Open minded
68. Confident
69. Assertive
70. Aware of your contribution

Glossary

Cabaret-style   Room layout where participants are seated around a room at small tables arranged around a central space, often in an arc or inverted U, to allow access by teachers/trainers to talk individually to groups.

Collaboration   Two or more individuals working together to achieve a common goal.

Contingency plan   A plan designed to take account of circumstances that might arise in the future, usually to avoid the failure of an activity.

Critical feedback   Responses that note quality aspects of a piece of work, including what was good and what could be improved.

DAC   The Development Assistance Committee is a forum to discuss issues surrounding aid, development and poverty reduction in developing countries.

Discovery research   Research that is at the cutting edge, usually of science and medicine, and usually results in products where the end-users have been involved in the discovery phase.

Disruptive (technology)   Innovative or ground-breaking (technology).

Doctoral College   Part of a university devoted to doctoral researchers as a focal point for a range of support and other services.

Doctoral training partnership   A model of funding doctoral researchers by bringing them together as a cohort for training and research purposes, usually involving more than one institution.

Engagement   Interactions with others through a variety of means including influencing and communicating verbally, visually, through text, sound, image and so on. Also see Public engagement.

Enterprise staff/office   The university staff who support the development of business or industrial applications of research knowledge.

Epistemic   Related to knowledge or the study of knowledge.

Ethics   The moral principles that guide and govern researchers' behaviour in the conduct of their research projects.

Evaluation:

> **Formative** Assessment of a learner's comprehension, academic progress and learning needs in order to provide feedback and guidance to aid improvement. Normally this occurs in-process, although it can be used by examiners at the end of a doctorate to guide future learning.

> **Summative** Assessment of a learner's progress at the end of a stage or a course in order to recommend onward progression to the next stage or an award to mark completion.

Feedback The range of comments and recommendations provided by assessors or evaluators in response to a piece of work they have been asked to judge.

Formative See Evaluation

Game-changer An idea or event or procedure that causes a significant shift in the current way of thinking about or doing something.

Gantt chart A chart to demonstrate which activities are to be performed when along a timeline.

HASS Short version of Humanities, Arts and Social Sciences.

Impactful In the case of research, this relates to a significant change made in something as a result of the research.

Imposter syndrome A pattern of behaviour in which people doubt the value of their accomplishments, often feeling a fear of being exposed as a fraud.

Inclusive culture The full and successful integration of diverse people in an organisation, event or situation.

Interdisciplinary Moving between or understanding of different disciplines within academia.

Interdisciplinary research Research that relates to more than one branch of knowledge. It crosses the nominal, artificial boundaries of disciplines or subjects so that knowledge and procedures from more than one discipline can be brought to bear on a problem.

Internships A period of work experience over a fixed time period for students or graduates to gain relevant skills and experience in a specific field. Companies assess the attributes of interns and frequently recruit them rather than advertising vacancies.

Inter-sectoral Moving between or understanding of different sectors in society.

Inter-sectoral research Research that crosses the nominal, artificial boundaries within society such as academia, industry, commerce, government, the health and social services sectors, and so on.

Knowledge Transfer Partnerships   A UK-wide programme that has for many years been helping businesses to innovate and grow by linking them with academic or research organisations and a graduate.

Narratives   Written or spoken accounts; representations of situations.

Norm   Something that is usual, typical or standard.

Outcome   The consequences of the research; its wider effect, which can be short or long term.

Output   In research, this equates to the results, conclusions, publications or products derived through the research.

Pedagogy   The method and practice of teaching.

Peer review   The process of evaluation of a piece of work by fellow scholars, groups of people within your scientific, academic or professional field, charged with maintaining standards. They provide feedback as well as decisions.

Placements   Structured programmes in which a student or postgraduate researcher spends a period, usually an academic year, working for an organisation as a full-time, paid employee to gain employability skills and experience before returning to university to complete a degree.

Praxis   The realising or enacting of a process.

Productive distractions   Term used by Dr Zoe Harris to describe activities that take you away from research work or physically prevent you from doing it (such as rock climbing) but are, nonetheless, useful and productive, especially good for mental health and well-being.

Professional doctorates   Internationally recognised doctoral programmes which consist of original research that contributes to both theory and practice in a specific professional field. Professional doctorates are especially common in health disciplines and some engineering disciplines.

Public engagement   The diverse ways that higher education institutions share their research, and the value of that research, with the public for mutual benefit.

Reflective practice   A method for developing self-awareness in a professional context. It involves critically thinking about one's actions with the aim of improving one's professional practice.

Research council   Government funding bodies for research focused on specific discipline areas. They were formerly grouped together as Research Councils UK (RCUK) but now come under the heading UK Research and Innovation (UKRI).

Researcher developers   University staff who provide a range of support for doctoral researchers, postdoctoral researchers and academic staff, specifically doctoral supervisors and examiners, and Principal Investigators/line managers.

Research Excellence Framework (REF) UK A five- to six-yearly UK national ranking of all higher education institutions to determine core funding. Ranking involves peer review of submissions not simply metrics such as research income, publications, citations, student numbers, the environment and impact. The process was reviewed by an independent authority, led by Lord Nicholas Stern: www.gov.uk/government/uploads/system/uploads/attachment_data/file/541338/ind-16-9-ref-stern-review.pdf

Root-and-branch approach A method or strategy which, when applied, has an effect on the entire system, organisation or a group, etc. that it is being applied to.

Sandpit A meeting that involves bringing together a group of people with knowledge in a specific area, or a range of areas, to discuss a specific research question or series of research questions.

Socratic method A method of questioning, developed by the Greek philosopher Socrates, designed to reach the heart of a topic. In the method, questions are continually asked about an assertion or an assumption until a contradiction is revealed. Exposure of this contradiction reveals that the initial assertion or assumption was erroneous.

STEMM An acronym to represent the disciplines Science, Technology, Engineering, Mathematics and Medicine.

Summative See Evaluation

Third space professionals University staff who fulfil roles that have academic and administrative aspects yet who fall into neither category but occupy a unique niche as boundaries blur, as defined by Celia Whitchurch.

Transactional relationships A connection or partnership between two parties that is of mutual benefit and where there is mutual exchange and reciprocity.

UKRI See Research council

Value added impact Impact that has increased in value as the result of development or improvement.

Index